2004 POETRY

ONCE UPON A RHYME

IMAGINATION FOR
A NEW GENERATION

Northern Surrey

Edited by Steve Twelvetree

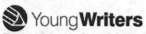 Young**Writers**

First published in Great Britain in 2004 by:
Young Writers
Remus House
Coltsfoot Drive
Peterborough
PE2 9JX
Telephone: 01733 890066
Website: www.youngwriters.co.uk

SB ISBN 1 84460 503 5

Foreword

Young Writers was established in 1991 and has been passionately devoted to the promotion of reading and writing in children and young adults ever since. The quest continues today. Young Writers remains as committed to engendering the fostering of burgeoning poetic and literary talent as ever.

This year's Young Writers competition has proven as vibrant and dynamic as ever and we are delighted to present a showcase of the best poetry from across the UK. Each poem has been carefully selected from a wealth of *Once Upon A Rhyme* entries before ultimately being published in this, our twelfth primary school poetry series.

Once again, we have been supremely impressed by the overall high quality of the entries we have received. The imagination, energy and creativity which has gone into each young writer's entry made choosing the best poems a challenging and often difficult but ultimately hugely rewarding task - the general high standard of the work submitted amply vindicating this opportunity to bring their poetry to a larger appreciative audience.

We sincerely hope you are pleased with our final selection and that you will enjoy *Once Upon A Rhyme Northern Surrey* for many years to come.

Contents

1st Halliford Brownies

Olivia Neary (7)   1
Rachel Adams (7)   1
Lucy Tucker (7)   1
Rebecca Ryan (8)   2
Bethany Maskell (8)   2
Chloe Baggs (8)   3
Emily Kemp (8)   3
Elizabeth Ellison (8)   3
Elizabeth Powell (8)   4
Beti Garside (8)   4
Megan Hedges (7)   4
Gemma Nangle (8)   4
Jessica Beagley (8)   5
Emily Robinson (8)   5
Ciara Thorpe (8)   5
Andrea Chisholm (9)   6
Lana Jagger (9)   6
Hayley Strong (9)   6
Sophie Baggs (10)   7
Laura Tucker (10)   7
Ella Brooks (9)   8

Burlington Junior School

Lauren Mallett (10)   8
Krishdga Sribala Krishnan (11)   9
Izzi Woodhouse   10
Kishaani Suseeharan   12
Ellie Ososki (11)   13
Victoria Bradley (11)   14
Jessica Mulopo (11)   15
Zoe Welch (11)   16
Tom Clark (11)   17
Sarah Heaton (10)   18
Meera Aldgarajah (11)   19
Haluk Ugur (11)   20
Aqeel Butt (11)   22
Sophie Freeman (11)   23
Sophie Stead (10)   24

Shaista Kerai (11)   26
Leanne North (11)   28
Bryn McGrath (10)   29

Clewborough House School
Luke Sodhi (9)   29
Stuart Hanvey (11)   30
Sofie Skouras (9)   30
Ankit Suri (10)   31
Nicola David (9)   31
Neil Hutchings (9)   32
Tim Aspinall (10)   32
Oliver Charles (9)   33
Cassandra Lazareff (10)   34
Thomas Cheyney (9)   35
Matthew Roberts (10)   36
Jordan Sturgess (9)   36
Katie Hill (10)   37
Ollie Brooke (9)   37
Matthew Carroll (10)   38
Russell Leung (10)   39
Luke Simpson (9)   40
Holly Alsop (10)   41
Stephanie Buzdygan (9)   42
Takahiro Moriyana (10)   43
Jessica Wilkins (10)   44
Joe Forrester (10)   45
Alexander Gresham-Thompson (10)   46

Gilbert Scott Junior School
Roberta Henriques (8)   46
Emily Goonetilleke (10) & Shanie Martin (9)   47
Tommy Greenwood (9)   47
Jade Falloon (10)   48
Richard Jenkins (11)   49
Luis Mendoza (8)   50

Hammond School
Georgina Lewis (9)   50
Georgina Longman-Turner (10)   51

Becky Lomax (10)   52
Molly Small (7)   52
Sarah Garmston (10)   53
Holly Tarling (9)   54
Gemma Horner (11)   54
Emily Smith (8)   55
Lucy Thorpe (11)   55

Purley Oaks Primary School
Liban (10)   56
Mark Akiwumi (11)   56
Melissa Miah (9)   57
Robert McQueen (10)   57
Natasha Wilson (11)   57
Jake Sherafatmand (9)   58
Ben Elliott (9)   58
Amina Matin (10)   59
Samuel Passman & Nathan Shaw (10)   60
Charlie Ell (8)   60
Hannah Louise MacDonald (10)   61
Frankie Wigger (10)   61
Jessica Clarke (9)   62
Alicia Hall (9)   62
Jordan Giddings (10)   63
Nadereh Alvani (10)   63
Peter Theobald (10)   64
Phillip Crawley (10)   64
Tinisha Ashley (11)   65
Nathaniel Bradshaw (10)   65
Paige Griffiths (9)   66
Zahrah Shah (9)   66
Danielle Clayden (10)   67
Rosie McGarry (8)   67
Aaliyah Binnie (8)   68
Harriet Fiddimore (9)   68
Emma Hallett (9)   69
Hannah Clarke (11)   69
Adam Hill (11)   70
Joshua Steventon (9)   70
Jenna Ram (8)   71
Daanish Shahid (8)   71

Ling Tang (9)   72
Joseph Blackwood (10)   72
Jacob Vibetti (10)   73
Robyn Payne (8)   73
Rebooca Harvey (10)   74
Louis Brixey (10)   74
Joanne Matheson (9)   75
Jessica Field (8)   75
Georgia Kelly (10)   76
Ken Robertson (10)   76
Vikki-Louise Parker (11)   77
Carl Shephard (11)   77
Katie Elliott (11)   78
Darcie Kelly (9)   78
Yasmeen Hussain (9)   79
Tahnée Seagrave (8)   79
Nicola Rogers (8)   80
Nazifa Hossain (8)   80
Tiana Hutton (11)   81
Lauren Ward (10)   81
Jessica Buswell (11)   82
Kirstie Rogers (11)   82
Callum McGerly, Alex Hill (9) & Charlie Kimber (10)   83
Abigail Mullins (11)   83
Kaitlyn Sheeran (9)   84
Gurpreet Ubi (8)   84
Charlotte Hedley (8)   84
Kainat Syeda (8)   85
Kelsey Stracey (9)   85
Lenina Aung-Mya (9)   86
Joel Livesley (8)   86
Lola Meredith (9)   87

St Anne's RC Primary School, Banstead

Chris Carr (9)   88
John O'Connor (8)   88
Katie Foster (7)   88
Niamh Carr (7)   89
Steven McNally   89
Emma Neil-Jones (8)   89
Clare Conway (8)   90

Louis Clarke (7)   90
Georgie Hobern (8)   90

St Luke's Primary School, Kingston
Fern Thomas (8)   91
Anna-Marie Lloyd (9)   91
Jenny Irving (8)   92
Ruby Mae Gibbs (8)   92
Katie L Hughes (8)   93
Sayed Adil Naziri (9)   93
Bella Horwood (9)   94
Josh Harris (9)   94
Elinor Anghileri (9)   95
Alice Foster (8)   95
Amelia Brown (8)   96
Ryan Wheeler (8)   97
Isabelle DuBois (8)   97
Henna Khan (8)   98
Jessica Dunne (9)   98

St Peter's Primary School, South Croydon
Elena Somovilla (10)   98
Trainette Gillam (9)   99
Emma Penn (9)   100
Louise Fallon (9)   100
Cherise Goode (10)   101
Esther Mullins (10)   101
Ruth Endersby (10)   102
Chloé Rushton (9)   102
Lauren Allam (9)   103
Laura Stone (9)   103
Samuel Taylor (9)   104
Poppy Nicholas (9)   104
Ciara Coleman (9)   105
Jodie Pain (11)   105
Alexandra Nicholls (9)   106
Jamie Askew (10)   106
Maria Christodoulides (10)   107
Joe Lobow (9)   107
Sarah Amrani (10)   108
Ariana Bravo (10)   108

Kerry Goodwin (10)   109
Stanley Payne (7)   109
Madeleine Wilson (7)   110
Mazvita Msemburi (7)   110
Tamara Bazil (11)   111
Naomi Taylor (10)   112
Bethany Baden (7)   113
Belen Tahir (10)   113
Sophie Ip (11)   114
Abigail Bates (11)   115
Joseph Kabbara (8)   115
Emma Tarrant (7)   116
Jason Ying (8)   116
Lucy Wordsworth (8)   117
Serena Williams (7)   118
Isabelle Wallin-Trapp (8)   119
Shannon Taylor (8)   120
Taban Stroude (8)   121
Amber Smith (7)   121
Ryan Sibbald (7)   122
Jordan Glass (7)   122
George Harman (7)   123
Samuel Lovell (7)   123
Gemma Dewhurst (7)   124
Iona Leigh (7)   124
Maryam Haque (7)   125

Stanley Park Junior School

Jamie Woods (9)   125
Claudina Vaz (9)   126
Bijal Shukla (9)   126
Lois Baker (9)   127
Eleanor Pullen (8)   127
Matthew Blow (10)   128
Daniel Browne (9)   129
George O'Neill (9)   129
Mark Richards (9)   130
Emine Sayan (8)   130
Harry Short (8)   131
Megan Harrison (10)   131
Jodie Atwell (9)   132

Jacob Ketcher (10)   132
Jasmine Rajagopalan (10)   133
Andrew Cross (10)   133
Rebecca Hall (9)   134
Katherine Woollett (8)   134
Shivani Rathod (9)   135
Joslyn Whiteman (9)   135
Thomas Grimes (10)   136
James Painter (9)   136
Sabrina Porter (10)   137
Onzo Izuchukwu (9)   137
Emma Holder (10)   138
Francesca Chapman (9)   138
Poppy Large (10)   139
Jade Le Gendre (9)   140
Suzanna Wells (9)   141
Thomas McDonald (11)   141
Victoria Constantinou (10)   142
Harry Frost (10)   142
Stephen Foss (10)   143
Louis Collingwood (11)   143
Lydia Murtezaoglu (10)   144
Hallam Rickett (10)   144
Kathryn Mossor (11)   145
Jonathan Davies (10)   145
Max Collins (10)   146
Paige Magorrian (8)   146
Eloise Bowden (8)   147
Laura McDonald (9)   147
Hollie Prentice (9)   148
Wayne Gyamfi (8)   148
Ben Harvey (10)   149
Olivia Guild (9)   149
Ben Hale-Jones (9)   150
Lisa Crow (9)   150
Samuel Gray (9)   151
Louis Ray (10)   151
Samantha Hall (9)   152
Taylor Felton (9)   152
Tim Brann (8)   153
James De Brunner (8)   153
Catherine Cheng (9)   154

Sean Reilly (9)   154
Nithin Thoppuram (8)   155
Lee Taylor (9)   155
Kerri Haines (9)   156
George Driscoll (9)   156
Georgina Howes (10)   157
Charlie Bone (10)   157
Ashley Gopee (10)   158
Francesca Newman (11)   158
Drew Beckley (11)   159
Kathryn Streatfield (10)   159
Brittany Edmondson-Jones (11)   160
Varuni Ponniah (10)   160
Jessica Harris (10)   161
Jake Gray (11)   161
Kiaran O'Leary (8)   162
Taha Maniar (9)   162
William Maclachlan (9)   163
Martha Ketcher (8)   163
Ben James (8)   164
Krishan Ganeshan (10)   164
Victoria Harding (8)   165
Sianna Lally (10)   165
Alexander Maclachlan (11)   166
Michael Short (10)   166
Robyn Glover (10)   167
Francesca Bailey (10)   167
Jessica Bourne (11)   168
Naran Maistry (9)   168
Amelia Hyatt (10)   169
George Fenner (11)   170
Karl Smith (10)   170
Max Harrison (11)   171
Stephen Rae (10)   171
Laura Gardner (10)   172
Gabriella Jeffery (11)   172
Adam Russell (10)   173
Stephanie Booth (11)   173
Sophie Smith (10)   174
Laura Neal (11)   174
Aimee Harwood (11)   175
James Jolley (11)   176

Chloe Robertson (11)   176
Eleanor Pryse-Hawkins (10)   177
Frankie Wood (10)   177
Charlotte Croucher (9)   178
Grace O'Leary (11)   178
Ashley Luckyram (9)   179
Lewis Farley (9)   179
Amie Steele (10)   180
Christopher Downing (10)   180
Cecily Snowball (10)   181
Daniel Haines (11)   181
Paul Staniforth (9)   182

The Mount Primary School
David Hitchin (8)   182
Pragash Rasalingam (8)   183
Elizabeth O'Connell (9)   184
Sian Hughes (8)   185
Georgia Bailey (10)   185
Regina Khan (10)   186
Zoë Davis (8)   186
Sam Besant (9)   187
Bethany Russell (8)   187
Sakshi Kumar (11)   188
Daniel Halawi (11)   188
Aman Bajaj (11)   189
Jason Pike (10)   189
Louise Thorne (10)   190
Kelly Neves (9)   191

The Raleigh School
James Tod (10)   191
Summer Dyason (11)   192
Daryl Thompson (10)   192
Louise Auld (11)   193
Megan Cook (9)   193
David Spratt (10)   194
Sam Holman-Hirst (10)   195
Elin Keyser (9)   195
Gemma Fraser (11)   196
James Fox (10)   196

Catherine Johnston (9)	197
Connor O'Hara (10)	197
Lucas de Carvalho (10)	198
Andrea Gould (9)	198
Rebecca Evans (10)	199
Megan Lane (9)	200
Robert Allott (11)	200
Kate Nicholls (7)	201
Hannah Punshon (10)	201
Nicholas Edwards (11)	202
Kate Penny (10)	202
Douglas Hampshire (10)	203
Dylan Brychta (11)	203
Robbie Kenny (10)	204
Katie Fuller (10)	204
Emily de Beaux (11)	205
Eleanor Johnston (8)	205
Kimberley Jarvis (11)	206
Catherine Roberts (10)	206
Olivia Flaherty (10)	207
Howard Jennings (7)	207
Stephanie Rendall (11)	208
Louise Patterson (10)	209
Jennifer Stonely (11)	209
Malin Stensson (11)	210
Oliver Carpenter (11)	211
Jonathan Nicholas (10)	211
Sarah Owens (10)	212
Lydia Charteris-Black (9)	212
Hallam Breen (8)	213
Kelly Brychta (9)	213
Dominic Barnes (9)	214
Emma Crighton (9)	214
Grace Cochran (10)	215
Matthew Penny (8)	215
Natalie Holroyd (10)	216
Niall Wright (9)	216
Yasmin Beckett (10)	217
Marcus Gilbert (9)	217
Niall O'Hara (8)	218
Dominic Carpenter (7)	218
Victoria Holloway (7)	219

Christie Dowling (7)   220
Verity Barnes (8)   220
Sophie Brindle (9)   221
Jessica Richardson (10)   221
Alexander Eller (9)   222
Clare Strange (9)   222
Christopher Hinchliff (10)   223
Zoe Light (10)   223
Charlie Powell (10)   224
Adam Knox (10)   224
Ailsa Keyser (9)   225
Sonia Smith (9)   225
Kiran Desor (10)   226
Daniel de Carvalho (8)   226
Harriet Lane (9)   227
Rebekah Lock (9)   227
Anna Flight (10)   228
Vanessa Rand (9)   228
Sam Maycock (9)   229
Emily Stanford (8)   229
Lewis Robinson (9)   230
Hetty Davies (9)   230
Joshua Tolley (9)   231
Alice Schaale (8)   231
Mary Lawton (9)   232
Dominic Hunt (9)   232
Amy Patching (8)   233
Hanna Greenstreet (8)   233
Rhiannon Davies (9)   234
Alex Davies (9)   234
Charlotte Merry (8)   235
Charlie Holland (10)   235
Tarun Aluvihare (9)   236
Jadesola Crundwell (8)   236
Amy de Beaux (8)   237
Zoella Zaborski (10)   237
Freya Bromley (9)   238
Anna Robinson (9)   238
Ellie Silvey (9)   239
Edward Baker (9)   239
Cameron Smith (8)   240

The Poems

Miss White

Miss White is a caring person
And she loves us all.
She has brown eyes and brown hair.
She is very kind and when I look at her
I think she isn't very old.
In fact she isn't very old,
But she is very bold.
That's my teacher Miss White!

Olivia Neary (7)
1st Halliford Brownies

The Rabbit

My little rabbit is soft and fluffy,
My little rabbit is black and white,
My little rabbit has a powder puff tail,
My little rabbit has long pointed ears,
My little rabbit has a small twitchy nose.
I love my little fluffy rabbit.

Rachel Adams (7)
1st Halliford Brownies

My Friend Jessica

My friend Jessica is very kind and nice,
She is very friendly and special to me
Jessica is very pretty,
And the best thing about Jessica
Is . . . she's my best friend!

Lucy Tucker (7)
1st Halliford Brownies

My Dog Jess

I have a dog
Her name is Jess,
She never lets me have a rest,
She wants to play,
She loves to walk,
I never get a chance to talk.

I take her to the local park,
We have to go when it's dark.
She loves to chase cats and dogs,
Even people out for a jog,
But I love her just the same,
Come on Jess let's have a game.

Rebecca Ryan (8)
1st Halliford Brownies

Dolphins

Dolphins
Leaping, twirling,
Twisting, turning,
Having fun,
Dolphins.
Spinning, playful,
Intelligent and blue,
Fantastic to watch,
Dolphins.

Bethany Maskell (8)
1st Halliford Brownies

My Big Sister Sophie

Kind, tall,
Blue eyes,
Clever and beautiful,
My big sister,
Sophie.

Chloe Baggs (8)
1st Halliford Brownies

My Dad

My dad is the best,
He is different from all the rest,
He's fun and cuddly,
He's lively and kind,
He's better than all the rest,
My dad is the best.

Emily Kemp (8)
1st Halliford Brownies

Kittens

Kittens.
Soft, fluffy,
Cute, small, playful,
The cuddly little things.
Kittens.

Elizabeth Ellison (8)
1st Halliford Brownies

Brownies

Brownies are
Kind, caring,
Loving, giving and sharing,
Wonderful to all,
Brownies have fun!

Elizabeth Powell (8)
1st Halliford Brownies

Caroline, My Best Friend

Caroline
Quiet, fun,
Blonde, caring, twin,
Plays with me and makes me happy,
Caroline.

Beti Garside (8)
1st Halliford Brownies

My Best Friend Emily

Emily is caring and sharing
She's pretty and funny,
She's really friendly,
And she's the best at being
Kind! Kind! Kind!

Megan Hedges (7)
1st Halliford Brownies

My Favourite Sweet

P erfect,
O range-shaped,
L ovely to eat
O n special occasions.

Gemma Nangle (8)
1st Halliford Brownies

My Best Friend

My best friend is
A nice person,
Dark blonde hair,
Hazel eyes,
Beautiful face,
A fun person.

My best friend is Lucy.

Jessica Beagley (8)
1st Halliford Brownies

Lauren!

Lovely, fantastic,
Beautiful, wonderful, funny,
She is so intelligent
That's Lauren.

Emily Robinson (8)
1st Halliford Brownies

Spice

Spice is very playful,
And she is very cheeky,
But she is cute and colourful,
She hides under the mat and is funny.
    She is my . . .
        Cat!

Ciara Thorpe (8)
1st Halliford Brownies

My Favourite Sweet

My favourite sweetie,
Yummy, scrummy,
Like a refreshment in my tummy,
Tasty and chewy,
Not at all gooey.

Andrea Chisholm (9)
1st Halliford Brownies

Mum

Mum
Caring
Loving
Pretty
I love her and she loves me
We are a *great* family.

Lana Jagger (9)
1st Halliford Brownies

My Sister Stephanie

Stephanie,
Loud, annoying, pulls my hair,
Bright blue eyes,
Hides food in my shoes,
Stephanie.

Hayley Strong (9)
1st Halliford Brownies

The Newcomer

'There's something new in the warren,'
The hare said as it hopped
It's got no fur, no floppy ears and no tail
And it cuddenly popped.

'There's something new in the sea'
The dolphin said as it floats.
It's got no gills, no skin or snout
And it ignores the massive boats.

'There's something new in the trees'
The blue tit said as it sang.
It's got no branches, no leaves nor roots,
And it suddenly went bang.

This poem is about a bomb
Landing in the environment.

Sophie Baggs (10)
1st Halliford Brownies

My Mummy

My mummy is loving,
My mummy is caring,
My mummy is nice,
Don't forget pretty!

My mummy can do everything,
She is the best.

My mummy is helpful,
My mummy is perfect,
My mummy is precious,
She shouts if I'm naughty.

That's my mummy!

Laura Tucker (10)
1st Halliford Brownies

Mum

Happy, funny,
Loving, kind, pretty
That's what my mum is like.

Ella Brooks (9)
1st Halliford Brownies

Jaok And The Beanstalk

Jack went to market to sell his cow,
Mum shouted 'You must sell her now.'
Don't sell poor Daisy very cheap,
Jack, you silly lazy creep.
Jack found a man to sell for a bean,
He looked so tall and very mean.

When Jack got back to show his mum,
She shouted, 'Surely not, you must be dumb!'
'Do you really mean you sold our Daisy for a bean?'
His mum chucked the bean with such a throw,
Not thinking how far it could possibly go.

The very next day when Jack went down,
His mum and him both gave a frown,
Because the bean had grown so high,
It reached right up into the sky.

Jack climbed the bean and gave a shout,
'I'm at the top without a doubt.'
A whole new world for him to see,
He met a giant whose name was Lee!

Lauren Mallett (10)
Burlington Junior School

Snow White

Once upon a time was a girl,
She liked to wear diamonds and pearls.
Her dream was to marry a handsome prince
Who liked to eat pies and mints.
The only problem that she had
Was her stepmother who drove her mad.
She looks in the mirror and says 'How are you?'
The mirror replies 'I'm fine thank you.'
But once she asked 'Who is the fairest?'
'Snow White of course is the rarest.'
'Go kill that girl,' she said.
'Whilst I rest in my comfy bed.'
'The woodcutter took Snow White to the Woods
He rose his axe and chopped her hood,
She ran away as fast as she could
Until she found a house made of wood.
'Oh my word, dwarves are here,'
'I don't believe the drink shaker.'
Her mother found out she was not dead,
She decided to do it herself instead.
Poison was put in a red juicy apple,
Then she got ready for the vicious battle.
Snow White ate the apple dead of course
Because she was playing how to divorce.
The prince came riding on his horse
Leaving his special driving course.
The curse will break
When Snow White awakes
On September the 20th when it's the eclipse
And true love brushes her lips.
Both will marry in a palace tall
And will live happily after all.

Krishdga Sribala Krishnan (11)
Burlington Junior School

Cinderella

Cinderella was a right tart
She was always one, right from the start.
She took her sister's boyfriends away
And put them in a sty of hay.

She kicked and punched her mum in the thigh
She did it until her mum started to cry.
One day a letter came
From up the hill and down the lane.

She opened it to herself
And hid it on the bathroom shelf.
The letter said 'Come to the ball,
But only if you're very cool.'

The Prince wants to find a bride
Who will stand by his side.
Cinderella got dressed
And didn't stop for a rest.

She put on a miniskirt
And then prepared to flirt.
She left without a single sound
And left in a hurry to be crowned.

In less time than she could say 'Boom'
She was standing in a crowded ballroom.
Drinking and drinking, never to stop
Suddenly she did a massive pop!

Everyone stopped
Everyone glared
Cinderella laughed
She wasn't at all scared.

Everyone joined in
Even the king
The Prince walked up to Cinderella
He was a charming, good-looking fella.

He smiled slowly
He got her a drink
Cinderella's breath
Began to stink.

He didn't kiss her, again
And Cinderella thought when, when, when
Will he ask me to marry him
Cinderella's chances were getting slim.

A little while later, the prince got near
And suddenly the prince gave a big cheer.
The prince said 'I have found a wife!
And I shall keep her for all my life.'

Cinderella jumped up
She couldn't believe it.
The Prince gave her a ring
She was happy to receive it.

And now let's sing our anniversary song
'No!' cried Cinderella 'I've been seeing another man!
I can't be with you,
Because I'm not your fan!'

Izzi Woodhouse
Burlington Junior School

The True Story Of Cinderella

Long, long ago there lived a girl named Cinderella,
She was the nicest girl in the land,
She'd never mind giving you a hand!
So the story starts at Cinderella's house,
She was looking at a photo of her mum (who died
ten years from this year)
When her dad tells her he's going to marry again,
but she had no fear,
Because she knew her dad would pick a wonderful
woman,
So the very next night her stepmother came,
It was quite obvious that her daughters wanted fame!
Cinderella's stepmother was very mean to her,
But behaved kindly towards Cinderella's dad,
She felt very, very sad,
Because she was being treated like a slave by her two
ugly sisters,
And they wouldn't be back very soon.
So she had to keep on cleaning up after the two ugly
sisters for a very long time,
Even when they went to dine,
Cinderella wasn't allowed to eat anything but the
leftovers!
One afternoon she'd just had enough
The two ugly sisters were too tough
Cinderella was crying very softly on the lawn
When suddenly she heard a horn
She looked up and saw her fairy godmother!
Cinderella was so shocked she just stared
Her fairy godmother asked her to get a pumpkin
that was teared,
Six white mice for horses, two lizards for the coachmen
and she made the pumpkin into a wonderful coach
She also made Cinderella a beautiful dress
Which hadn't a bit of mess

After all Cinderella got to go to the ball
She married the handsome prince
And lived happily every after
But the ugly sisters, they're another story!

Kishaani Suseeharan
Burlington Junior School

Sleeping Beauty
(I bet you don't know the real story)

Sleepy was dancing with the prince, when all of a sudden
She started to wince.
She fell down on the floor
And admitted the prince was a terrible bore.
Sleepy fled and left the scene
She didn't want to be classed as mean.
She went off to her mumsie's home
Where they were very poor and as thin as a bone.
Sleepy demanded more and more
She didn't want to be skinny and poor.
So she walked out of the red door
So Sleepy went to the bar
Where they were dancing the cha, cha, cha.
She fell in love with Mr World -
Who was ugly and terrible and always smelled.
They were married straight away
And it's their 60th anniversary on this day.

Ellie Ososki (11)
Burlington Junior School

Cinderella

Once there was a little girl
And the sight of her made you hurl
Her brown suitcase, her
blistered face and her manky
greasy hair.
One day whilst eating toast
An invitation came through
the post
'To the ball I go for me for me
But I must not let my sisters
see.'
Later that night she pottered
round the house quieter than a
mouse then left the house
without a sound
Then off to the disco she went,
entrance fee £1.00.

Later that night with the
music thud, under the disco
light sat Cinderella by the door
when something went a rolling
on the floor.

Picking up the coin she took
herself off to buy another
drink.
But 1, 2, 3, of a blink, a fairy
appeared dressed in pink.
'What will your wish be?' said
the fairy
'I want the prince to marry me,'
replied Cindy.
'If this is your wish it will do,
the prince will surely marry you.'

So she asked the prince and he
said 'I do.'
Now they're together and
living as two.

Victoria Bradley (11)
Burlington Junior School

Sleeping Ugly

Sleeping ugly
Wasn't funny
Didn't say
She couldn't play
She pricked her finger
In a wager
So she fell asleep
Without a peep
She couldn't be woke
Without a poke
Unless he wore a royal cloak
The prince came
With a blazing flame
He became her mate
They went out for a date
And he wasn't late
For their romantic date.

Jessica Mulopo (11)
Burlington Junior School

Little Red Riding Hood

There once was a cottage on a hill
Which had a lovely water mill
The people who lived there were so bad
They made all the neighbours really mad
The child there was so mean
I'm telling you her skin was green
One day her mum asked her to
Go down to Granny's and give her a few
Biscuits and cakes cos she has a sweet tooth
So off Red went to see Granny Ruth
On her way she tripped and fell
Over a magic wishing well
She wished the wolf would not appear
She did not want to walk in fear
When she arrived at the tatty old house
Her granny was there as safe as a mouse
'Oh no what's happened?' Red said
'What's happened to your beautiful head?
And your feet they're so tiny and small
In fact they're hardly there at all.'
'Don't worry I'll be back to normal soon
Tell me dear when's the next moon?'
'You're a mouse is it really true?'
'Yes I am but it's just between me and you'
'Oh the full moon of course it's next week'
'What happens then Granny? Tell me please speak.'
'I'll turn back to normal like I was'
'Why does it happen? Is it because
When you were little your dream was to be
A beautiful white mouse as happy as can be?'
'Yes I'm afraid you've found me out
My wish went wrong and now I've got a snout.
You'd better go now it's getting quite late'
'OK Granny I'll go play with my mate.'

Zoe Welch (11)
Burlington Junior School

Jack And The Beanstalk

Jack was a boy who was very dumb
He wasn't very well so he kept sucking his thumb.
His mum said to him 'Go and sell that cow
She's been here longer than I have now.'

To prove that Jack was not lazy
He set off early to go and sell Daisy.
He met a man who seemed very nice
He gave Jack some magical beans as the price.
When Jack got home to show Mum the beans,
She got very annoyed and wasn't too keen.
She grabbed hold of Jack and gave him a clout
Took the beans and threw them out.
Over the night a beanstalk grew
It grew higher than the birds flew.
Jack started to climb and didn't look down
The house looked tiny and so did the town.
Above was a castle big and wide
Jack opened the door and stepped inside.
He saw a large table with a book and a pen
And right by its side was an odd-looking hen.
The hen gave a squawk at Jack
Jack grabbed the hen and put her into a sack
He ran and he climbed back down and wondered
He heard a loud bang that thundered
Jack looked above and saw an enormous shoe
It belonged to a large giant, what was he to do?
'Go get the axe' he called to his mum.
She came running quickly and asked 'What have you done?'
He chopped at the beanstalk as hard as he could
It came crashing down on the shed made of wood
The giant lay dead, Jack beamed with pride
He grabbed the hen and took it inside
It gave a squawk and laid an egg made of gold
They bought back Daisy and that's the story told.

Tom Clark (11)
Burlington Junior School

Little Red Riding Hood

One day Red Riding Hood
Asked her mum if she could
Go visit old Grandmamma
And take Gran's favourite choccy bar
So she set off and on the way
I will tell you if I may, she
Met a very ugly old man
Who hit her with a frying pan
She had told him where she was going
Over the river the one still flowing
So meanwhile the old man raced on
And in a few seconds he was gone
When she woke up she set off again
Later she reached Gran's cottage and then
Knocked on the little wooden door
Matching the polished wooden floor
Someone looking like Gran answered her call
Then she realised it wasn't Gran at all
She decided not to let the old man know
And that she would just go with the flow
The man sat down in Gran's favourite chair
Acting like Gran was dead and he was her heir
She said 'Granny what big teeth you've got!'
He said 'All the better to eat you . . . *What!*'
. In came the police and grabbed the man
And drove him away in their old van
She searched the house and found Grandma
And gave her her favourite choccy bar.

Sarah Heaton (10)
Burlington Junior School

Snow White

Once upon a time there lived a rich king,
who proposed to a wicked witch with a ring.
They got married the very next day,
and had a child born on the 1st of May.
Snow White was the name of the child,
who grew up to be calm and mild.
Every day the vain witch would call
to the golden mirror on the wall
She cried 'Mirror, mirror on the wall,
who is the fairest of them all?'
'You are,' the mirror replied
As it turned away and sighed.
Princess Snow White turned eighteen
When terrible news was proclaimed to the queen
She bellowed 'Mirror, mirror on the wall,
who is the fairest of them all?'
The mirror had a smile on its face,
and said 'Snow White has taken your place.'
The enraged queen yelled and howled
And called for the huntsman who emerged and bowed
The witch shrieked, 'Destroy that ugly brat
or I shall turn you into a smelly rat!'
She ordered him to kill the lovely Snow White,
in the middle of the cold dark night.
The assassin set off with a sharp axe in hand,
and found Snow White playing in golden sand.
He led the princess into the dark woods,
And raised his axe as high as he could.
He struck her with a mighty blow
and saw the river of blood flow
The princess was lying in a pool of red,
and the lovely Snow White was dead!

Meera Aldgarajah (11)
Burlington Junior School

Cindy And The Three Bad Wolves

Once upon a time on a sunny day,
Cinderella was cleaning all the way,
She had to do the washing,
She had to do the shopping,
She had to do the tidying,
She had to do the mopping,
Suddenly there was someone at
the door,
She approached it but only saw,
Her sisters in fancy clothes,
Even wearing a bright red rose.
'Cinderella you smell like a trout,
I order you to move out!'
Cinderella walked out with
pleasure,
And thought that she could earn
treasure.
But then they warned her 'Beware!
There are evil things out there!'
There was a builder named Bob,
Selling bricks was his job.
She asked the builder for some
bricks for free,
He replied yes and gave loads to Cindy.
She built her house of bricks
Not straw, not wood not even sticks.
Cindy heard noises like thump,
thump, thump.
She looked up and saw three bad
wolves in a grump.
The leader ordered to have her house
smashed,
Cindy saw the back door and ran and
dashed.
Cinderella found a rhino and nicked
some concrete,
The rhino didn't notice 'cause he was
eating meat.

When she finished she ran inside,
'Cause the wolves were there and she
went to hide.
The leader said 'You better run.
Come on boys let's have some fun.'
They tried and tried to drill the house
down,
But stopped and gave a wondering frown
Because Cindy had a weapon in her hand,
Which would blow the three bad
wolves into sand.
But Cindy was so scared she ran into
the back door
And the wolves picked the weapon and
blew the front door,
But when they walked in the walls were
like squash,
Gone forever in the wash,
And Cinderella lived in peace
With her lovely adorable niece.

Haluk Ugur (11)
Burlington Junior School

Jack And The Beanstalk

'Jack' said his mum 'You're very, very lazy
Go and sell our cow Daisy.'
Soon Jack met a very smelly man,
Who said 'I'll swap that cow for some beans in a can.'

When Jack told his mum what he swapped for the cow
She turned bright red and screamed 'You're a stupid old sow.'
She grabbed the bean and flung it out
And when it landed it started to sprout

Then with such a force that could knock down a horse
She beat the boy for an hour and a half.
She hit him with a bottle of rum
And he went to sleep with a sore bum.

He woke up next morning
Tired and yawning
He saw the bean tall and high,
It was almost as tall as the sky.

Jack started climbing up and up
Until he reached the mighty top.
Then he saw a giant castle
And hid in the giant's parcel.
Then he saw the huge giant
Boy was he a mean tyrant.

The giant said 'Please come in'
Then Jack saw the giant's bride standing next to the bin.
Jack ran away with the giant's bride
While the giant cried and cried.
Jack's wife said 'Go and steal the giant's gold, he surely has got
quite a lot.'
So Jack went to the giant's castle and hid all the gold inside
a pot.

The giant spotted Jack running out of his house
He was as quiet as a mouse.
Jack started climbing down to the ground
Then he heard a thundering sound.
'Fee fie foe fum, I'll squish Jack between my huge thumb.'

So the giant started climbing down and down
While Jack had reached the ground
He started chopping
While his wife was mopping
The stalk started falling down to the ground
Then the giant fell and died, and all the people gathered round.

They all came to see the first ever giant
They all agreed that he was a terrible tyrant.
So Jack and his wife lived happily ever after
And their house was always filled with laughter.

Aqeel Butt (11)
Burlington Junior School

Jack And The Beanstalk

Jack was a very poor boy
He only had just one toy
His mum was very poor
Everything was broken, even the door
Jack's Mother said,
'Time to get out of bed.
It's time to sell our pig.'
Jack sold his pig for a fig,
His mum threw the fig out
With a moan and a shout,
First thing in the morning
When the day was dawning
A beanstalk of food did grow,
Up Jack did go,
At the top a giant stood,
Wearing a coat and hood,
He chased Jack back down,
Jack he did frown,
Jack ate all the food he found,
The giant fell to the ground.
Jack could sleep nice in his bed
Knowing the giant was dead.

Sophie Freeman (11)
Burlington Junior School

Jack And The Bean

This story is so hard to tell
It all depends on how to sell
The story is Jack and the bean
His mother was so very mean.

One day his mum asked if he could go
And sell their cow called Billyo
So he set off to sell the cow
But he thought to himself *How? How? How?*

He went straight to the market
To sell her for something hard to get
When he arrived back in the afternoon
His mum said
'You're back so soon'

'Look Mumsy dear guess what I got?
Some lovely beans in a pot?'
'Oh Jack you stupid boy
For a week you'll have no toys!'

And with that she threw them out the
window
And said to herself,
'That'll teach him so.'
The very next day the beans had grown
And in the sun it was really shown.

He climbed up the bean till he reached the
top
He looked around then looked up and
stopped
He gave a cry, it was the giant
He ran around and caused a riot.

Jack begged and begged to let him go
But the giant replied
'No, no, no'
The giant said,
'You'll be my snack
Before I take my afternoon nap.'

Jack ran and ran till he got away
And the giant shouted to him
'You'll have to pay'
Jack ran till he reached the castle
And outside the door was a parcel
He picked up the parcel and swung it about
And said to himself
'This is full of trout.'

He crawled under the door and found some
gold
And said
'That's too heavy to hold.'
He stuffed the gold in his pockets
And was out of the castle like a rocket.

He climbed back down the stalk
As if he was flying like a hawk
He had so much gold I swear
That he was an instant millionaire.

Sophie Stead (10)
Burlington Junior School

Three Bad Wolves And A Cheeky Cinderella

Once a girl called Cinderella,
Whose bedroom was a slimy cellar,
Was cleaning up her sisters' house,
When sister one (she's like a mouse),
Came up to her and snarled, 'You girl!'
Cindy turned with a twirl.
She replied, 'You little croop.'
Her sister then began to weep.
Sister two hollowed, 'Out now!'
Cinderella was gone with a *pow*.

Down the path she walked along,
Her feet sticky and beginning to pong,
She met a builder named Bob,
Who was extremely rubbish at his job.

She asked politely, 'May I have some bricks?
Or wood, or straw, or even sticks?'
Not bothered he yawned, 'No way Jose.
'Please could you go away?'
She gave poor Bob a gigantic whack
And lifted the bricks onto her back.

In less than a day her house was made,
And on her bed her head she laid.
Lost in dreams Cinderella slept,
Whilst the three bad wolves slowly crept,
They stood by the house and counted to three,
The chief shouted 'Knock it down, haa, haa, hee, hee.'

In the nick of time Cinderella ran out,
She looked at her house and began to pout,
'Talk about a housewarming,
They didn't even bother to ring.'

Puzzled, Cindy found a rhino
He was selling cement and coloured lino.
'Rhinoceros sir, may I have some cement?'
'No, no my dear, I'd rather you went.'
She gave the poor rhino a gigantic whack,
And carried the cement away on her back.

In less than a day her house was made,
And on her bed her head she laid.
Lost in dreams Cinderella slept,
Whilst the three bad wolves slowly crept.
They stood by the house and counted to three,
The chief shouted 'Drill it down, haa, haa, hee, hee.'

But the force rebounded and Cindy said
'I won't give up. Why don't you instead?'
She ran out the back door to find a gun,
Where she found the gunseller's son.
She stole a gun and screeched 'Pay you back.
Sorry, no time to slack.'

When she got home the wolves were still there,
The walls were still firm with no need for repair.
She held up her gun but dropped it in terror,
Her stupidity she will remember forever.

She ran into the house and out of the door,
Her feet were now very sore.
They shot after the girl, but they hit the wall,
And on top of them the house began to fall.

Cinderella is now as happy as can be,
And the wolves are in Heaven, yes all three.

Shaista Kerai (11)
Burlington Junior School

Jack And The Beanstalk

Jack went to market to sell the cow.
At least sell it for one hundred pounds,
Jack goes, 'I will go to Dean,
And get those wicked beans.'
Jack went home to show his mum,
His mum shouted 'You are so dumb.'
Jack went to his room in a mood,
Because there wasn't any food.

The very next day when Jack went down
His mum and him both gave a frown,
'Cos the bean had grown so high,
It went right up into the sky.
Jack went out to climb the bean,
And saw the giant that was mean.

'What's your name?' Jack asked the giant.
'My name's Dean, *get off my bean.*'
Jack went down to tell his mum,
The giant bowed and said 'Yum, yum.'
The giant turned round and saw the mighty bean
It was on the floor.
Dean moved in and married Jack's mum,
They didn't live in a ditch,
Cos they became, so very rich.

Leanne North (11)
Burlington Junior School

Little Red Riding Hood

'Little Red' said Mum 'Take these supplies
to Auntie Wolf to make her wise,
but beware oh yes, of the bad Granny
for it will make her very happy,
to find a young girl in the forest.'
So off she went to pass the florist,
but on the way the granny she passed
and told her that she had a cast,
so the granny said 'Well walk with me
but if you don't you are silly.'
'Thank you but no thank you' said Little Red,
'These pills have to get to Auntie's head.'
So off she went once more again
and arrived at Auntie's at half-past ten,
but looked around there was no wolf there
except for someone with a bundle of hair
So Little Red pulled out a gun
and shot this suspicious someone.

Bryn McGrath (10)
Burlington Junior School

The River

The river is flowing very fast
It's coming from the top of the hill
Soon it will reach the waterfall
Then it will fall
Crashing down on the rocks
To meet the lake at the bottom
Slowly now it will move gracefully on.

Luke Sodhi (9)
Clewborough House School

What Is Home?

What is home? I have no idea,
It all just seems like a mixed up dream.
What is home? The wind and the breeze
What is home? My brain seems to freeze.

What is Africa? Mummy please tell,
Tell me the plains, that burnt up your tail.
What is the wasteland? Please let me know,
What is Africa? What is home?

Now we are captured and all locked away,
Can you tell me what happened day after day.
Did you work or did you grow?
What is Africa? What is home?

For our last days, what shall we do?
Shall we be happy, or shall we be blue.
There is the zoo keeper, coming this way,
Shall we stay here or shall we run away?
Mummy don't go, I'll be all alone,
What is Africa? What is home?

Stuart Hanvey (11)
Clewborough House School

Vitava

Tributaries trickle down the peaceful river, down
the relaxed river, the river's flowing faster.
The river is dashing, turning and flashing.

Now the river is getting slower the river is turning
into the corners.
The river is trickling slower and slower.

The river is now getting faster, the river is falling down
a waterfall, swishing tapping and jumping.
The river can feel the fish jumping and dancing.

The river is now joining into the sea now the river is free.
The river is swimming out far out to the open sea.

Sofie Skouras (9)
Clewborough House School

The River's Journey

The river begins its journey
Down and down it goes
City to city town to town
Slowly and merrily it flows.

Giving fish a home
Playing with the rocks
Creating all that foam
Going past the ducks.

Speeding through the rapids
Running down the falls
Joining the sea
As it hears its calls.

Ankit Suri (10)
Clewborough House School

Guss Hail

Who throws squares
down to make
you go pale?

Guss Hail.

Who freezes you
and you really want
to bite your nail?

Guss Hail.

Who makes you
stay at home but you
want clothes from the sale?

Guss Hail.

Who makes the roads
slippery and you can't
get out for a test and you fail?

Guss Hail.

Nicola David (9)
Clewborough House School

Journey Of The River

From humble beginnings
Trickling down as a stream
Joining up with others now
It goes faster
Rushing and gushing
Now it's a river.

Flowing, growing, exploring
That is what it does now
It is loving the ravine
While it falls it thinks of
Where it will land.

While it's flowing and shining
Through a marvellous town
Everyone notices it
In the gleaming sun.

Neil Hutchings (9)
Clewborough House School

Tim Rain

Who bangs on your door
Like someone insane?
Tim Rain.
Who sneaks down the lane?
Tim Rain.
Who whips you like a cane?
Tim Rain.
Who looks like a chain
And slithers down the drain?
Tim Rain.
Who soaks you through and makes you complain?
Tim Rain.

Tim Aspinall (10)
Clewborough House School

James Hurricane

Who keeps
all kids at home
being a pain?
James Hurricane.

Who breaks
homes as they
tag with rain?
James Hurricane.

Who throws
all away
as he runs down the lane?
James Hurricane.

Who drives
most of the
kids insane?
James Hurricane.

Who stops
you as
you fly on a plane?
James Hurricane.

Who has a
quest to make
everything impossible to obtain?
James Hurricane.

Oliver Charles (9)
Clewborough House School

River Poem

Tiny little drops of water glistening in the sun,
Fall from the glacier,
They all rush in teamwork
To form the . . . river.

Through the winding bends,
Over the rocks and stones,
Watching the cattle in the fens,
I wander on and feel alone.

I whoosh and I splash and I ripple and I tinkle,
I glisten and I shine and I sparkle and I twinkle,
I mumble and I tumble and I rumble along
Listen to me now as I chant my river song.

I rush down the hillside, I whisper to my neighbour,
I watch a child play with her colourful kite,
I relax in the sunshine while the raindrops push me
to and fro,
I sing along the mountainside, I enjoy myself so.

My journey comes to an end,
I say goodbye to my friends,
I pour into the sea,
As nature waves goodbye to me.

Cassandra Lazareff (10)
Clewborough House School

The River

The river starts creeping
Slowly peeping
Around a stone
All alone.

Trickling, tumbling
Tickling, stumbling
Down the dips
It trips and slips.

To the deep ravine
A dark and muddy scene
It travels boldly
Clear and coldly.

Flowing faster
Onwards past a
Well used ford
And on toward

A waterfall
Grand and tall
Splashing, spraying
Sunlight playing.

As it slows
It really grows
Getting bigger
With a snigger.

It goes out into the sea.

Thomas Cheyney (9)
Clewborough House School

My River Poem

As the stream flowed down the mountain
It splashed and gurgled like a fountain.
The wet rocks sparkled in the sun
All the otters are having fun.
The fish swim under rocks to hide
While the fisherman looks from side to side.
On the bridge were mountain bikers
Talking with a group of hikers.
On a boat some people laughed
And waved at others as they passed.
The men found it really hard to row
Because of the river's heavy flow.
It goes back to the sea
It was a lovely journey for me.

Matthew Roberts (10)
Clewborough House School

The Dashing River

By the dashing river
the water splashes by,
rushing rapids bashing
against the rocks,
the water goes up high.

The water's flowing quickly,
smashing as it goes,
rushing past the fisherman's toes,
off the river goes.

The river's going high,
nearly touching the sky,
it had found its way
by the end of the day,
down the waterfall.

Jordan Sturgess (9)
Clewborough House School

River Poem

The river flowing gently into the sea
The trickling sound of water I can hear
Fish are jumping in and out flying
Happily in and out of the river.

The water rushing over the rocks
Hearing the sound of pebbles crash
Children splashing and dashing in and out
Of the water and shouting with glee.

People celebrating, having barbecues near the river.
People are fishing and dishing food out,
While the river goes blue and shiny
And travelling slowly watching.

Now the river is going much slower and sadder
When it makes its way back to sea.
Goodbye old river,
There is a whole new world waiting for you.

Katie Hill (10)
Clewborough House School

Journey Of The River

As the river starts spinning
On the rocky path getting bigger and bigger
As it gets to the bottom of the mountain
Stronger and faster over the rocks.

It winds its way down the valley
Deeper and darker and bringing life to the land.
Full of fish and furry creatures.

Winding faster, deeper, stronger.
Flowing down to the sea where it meets the
Crashing waves, a spectacle for all to see.

Ollie Brooke (9)
Clewborough House School

The River Journey

Some water trickles slowly out of a spring, and down the
mountainside.
The stream gets bigger and bigger
and turns into a river roaring down the
mountainside.
The river is pushing and pulling at all the
things that get in its way.

The river gets to a deep ravine
deeper and darker than the river has ever been.
It must keep going faster and faster as if it's
going to a drop.

The rapids are quick the rapids are bendy.
The river cannot stop; it can see the drop the river cannot stop.

The river is getting faster, faster and faster.
Suddenly the river falls down, down, down, down, smash.

The river sprints away from the waterfall to a calm bend.
The river can see a village at its banks
The river looks up and reflects the clouds in the sky.

The river can see the city it has been trying to get to.
The river feels proud.

Matthew Carroll (10)
Clewborough House School

Journey Of A River Vitava

Tributaries trickle
Down to the mountains
Tributaries down and fast and
Rushing to the Prague.

River trickling, flowing
In peacefully,
Calm and exploring to
The Prague.

People dancing, fishing in the summer.
Calm and peaceful.
The river sliding
To the forest.

The forest was mean
And scary.
If you explore in
You will turn evil
And scary.

Finally the river arrived
At the Prague, into
The Grand Park
In the city.

Russell Leung (10)
Clewborough House School

Dance Of The River Haiku

Tributaries will
join rapidly and often
making quite a team.

Now the river's born
flowing down the mountainside
getting really rough.

Getting faster by
the steady, coming seconds
water's really white.

Very wide and fast
going over the rapids
it passes some hunts.

It passes through a trench
and comes very close to
a deep waterfall.

The water falls fast
down over some craggy rocks
it crashes harshly.

Tired and worn out
the river winds into the
ocean and is done.

Luke Simpson (9)
Clewborough House School

The River's Journey

The river begins its journey
As a stream it has far to go
Towards the gushing water
It twists and turns down eagerly.

Sparkling proudly in the glistening sunshine
Lazing around the river banks
People dance and have picnics
While the river parades in glory.

Moving towards the waterfall
Faster and faster the river can't stop
Crashing and fighting in the great big war
Relieved he's got through
He carries on amazed

Through a tunnel calm and peaceful
Dark and cold, pitch-black
Out the other side the wondrous river goes
Slowly past a village he flows through.

Holly Alsop (10)
Clewborough House School

River Journey Poem

First the river starts flowing
You don't have to pay
The river will always be growing
Every single day.

Next, the water gets dancing,
Over every rock
Every time it goes to prancing,
It's like it's in a talk.

Then the rapids come
In a great, huge rush,
All in one big huddle,
It's one big brush.

It comes to a deep ravine
It's never been here before,
It's darker than we've ever seen,
I'll go here a lot more.

It's gone to the waterfall
It's right at the top
It's like a very big pool
Now it's at the . . . *drop!*

Finally it's at the end,
It feels very proud,
People are cheering,
It's a very big crowd.

Stephanie Buzdygan (9)
Clewborough House School

The River's Journey

The river starts with its source
Now the little streams make a course
To make a river and starts the journey
Now It's starting to flow.

They're jumping hopping
Down the mountainsides
Trying to get to the bottom
As fast as it could.

The river is starting to sparkle
While the flow gets faster
The rocks are getting in the way
Crashing gushing to the end.

Turning, twisting it's going wild
Bursting, bubbling it's going crazy
Now it's reached it's about to drop
It's falling fast until it lands.

It's still skipping
And of dancing
It's still happy
And still running.

Now it's in a ravine
But still won't stop
Now it's in a rapid
It's starting to lose control.

Now it's resting
So it can run smoothly
Now it's slowly waking
Trying to get into shape.

Now it's gliding and sliding
And no more jogging
Now it's springing as fast as it could
He's on his last ten metres and he's past the goal.

Takahiro Moriyana (10)
Clewborough House School

Apple Pie Poem

A was an apple
B borrowed it
C cooked it
D diced it
E enjoyed it
F fried it
G glazed it
H halved it
I ignored it
J juiced it
K kicked it
L licked it
M munched it
N nibbled it
O observed it
P peeled it
Q questioned it
R rolled it
S squashed it
T tormented it
U used it
V viewed it
W washed it
X x-rayed it
Y yelled at it
Z zipped it.

Jessica Wilkins (10)
Clewborough House School

Apple Pie Poem

A was an apple pie
B borrowed it
C cooked it
D dated it
E enjoyed it
F was frightened of it
G guarded it
H hated it
I inspired it
J juggled it
K kissed it
L labelled it
M mothered it
N nursed it
O ordered it
P played with it
Q quizzed it
R raced it
S smelt it
T transported it
U unsettled it
V volleyed it
W wrecked it
X x-rayed it
Y yearned for it
Z zipped it.

Joe Forrester (10)
Clewborough House School

Sam Sun

Who makes you sweat
And boil
That you have no fun?
Sam Sun.

Who's always there in the daytime
But not in the night-time
So it scares your son?
Sam Sun.

Who does not make
You cold as ice
But as hot as a roast bun?
Sam Sun.

Who stops you going
Scouts pace
Jog and run?
Sam Sun.

Alexander Gresham-Thompson (10)
Clewborough House School

The Train To Manchester

Here is the train to Manchester,
Here is the train to Edinburgh,
The wheels of the train are going round and round,
While I'm sitting not make a sound.
The train is collecting many, more people,
Meanwhile I'm eating strawberry treacle.
At last I've got to Manchester,
Goodbye train to Edinburgh.

Roberta Henriques (8)
Gilbert Scott Junior School

Dancing Horses

Shooting stars are white horses,
Galloping throughout all of space.
Making their way through the darkest nights,
Silent and hard to trace.

Swiftly moving through the galaxy,
Dancing past the Milky Way,
'Til he finds his place to sleep,
He sleeps throughout the day.

Emily Goonetilleke (10) & Shanie Martin (9)
Gilbert Scott Junior School

I Remember

I remember. . .
When I was small,
The first time ever,
I kicked a ball.

I remember. . .
A few years gone,
It was so funny
I fell in the pond.

I remember. . .
Just last year
Jack nearly drowned
I had no fear.

I remember. . .
A few hours ago
My little brother said
'My tooth's starting to grow'
I wonder what I'll remember tomorrow.

Tommy Greenwood (9)
Gilbert Scott Junior School

Lessons In Action!

And there goes the whistle in the playground for the beginning
of the day.
Science is first lesson of the day with loads of energy.
>Experiment,
>Chemicals,
>Explosions!

English is still holding for dear life as it struggles to try and
beat Science, still looking very moody.
>Stories,
>Poems,
>Playscripts.

Science is getting very angry as energetic English keeps elbowing
Science out of the way.
>Pointy pencils,
>Blunt sharpeners,
>Pens out of energy.

Ah, it's now break time and it's looking bad for Science today.
It is now the end of break time and it's mega maths turn
to try and get to the top of the popularity list and he's off.
>Calculators,
>Subtraction,
>Numbers.

Mega maths is first now, English has gone down to second place
and poor science has been knocked down to third place,
whinging and moaning.
And that's the end of the day.
I suppose we'd better be going now. Bye!

Jade Falloon (10)
Gilbert Scott Junior School

The Battle Of The Subjects

That's the bell for the start of the day and science looks very energetic.
It wants prime time teaching today.
Chemicals, life forms,
Microscopes, explosions.

Maths is in the ring, juggling numbers everywhere.
Science throws a chemical jar at Maths,
But Maths deflects it back, it's not going to be beaten.
Shapes, times tables,
Fractions, nasty numbers.

And that's the end of Science for the day.
He's not pleased!
Here's Playtime running around like a child.
Football, tennis,
Running, shouting,
Back to lessons PE first.

Fit as a runner is PE, beat anyone in a race he could.
Gymnastics, dance,
Rugby, fitness.

History comes out now, looking very old.
But don't underestimate him.
Tudors, Stuarts,
Victorians, Romans.

Ding! The final bell.
Everyone's gone home;
We'd better go too.
Goodbye!

Richard Jenkins (11)
Gilbert Scott Junior School

Smelly Trainers

Please don't throw me old trainers away,
Not today please Mama not today.

I love those trainers yuh can tell,
Because they've got a real powerful smell!

If you throw me trainers away today,
I won't come out of me room to play.

I'll be so sad, I'll get so moany,
You mustn't throw them away.

I'll make yuh a promise I sure to keep,
How about if I do de washing up for a week?

Oh dear Mama I can see you're mad,
But in the end yuh be so glad!

Luis Mendoza (8)
Gilbert Scott Junior School

Rainbow

R ainbow, rainbow way up high,
A iming for the top of the sky,
I nside or outside you can see it,
N aming all of the colours of it,
B elow there is a pot of gold,
O thers don't believe this,
W ill you?

Georgina Lewis (9)
Hammond School

Can You Find The Love?

I wake up,
I feel something is missing,
Do you feel it too?
It's the love for one another,
It is no more,
It can come back,
At least I hope so.
There is an empty space,
Meant to be full of love,
Do you feel it too?
I look under a stone . . .
No,
I look under a boulder . . .
No,
I look under a house . . .
No.
I lift an earring . . .
Yes.
It is so small, oh,
Oh what have we done to our world,
Oh what have we done to our homes,
We must bring back the love,
Before it is lost completely.
Please let it come back
We can get the love back but only together . . .

Georgina Longman-Turner (10)
Hammond School

Night

Night is a devil,
Night has red skin,
Night has bright blue eyes,
Night has slits for a nose,
Night has hairy legs,
Night has spiky horns on his head,
Night jumps and runs in the dark,
Night lives in a gloomy cave,
Night eats raw fich,
Night is a horrid creature,
Night makes spooky noises that make me quiver,
Night is a thing I wish to avoid,
Night is coldblooded,
Night makes me feel sad,
Night makes good things turn bad,
Night has habits that are horrid,
Night hates daylight,
Night is evil,
Night is a devil.

Becky Lomax (10)
Hammond School

Dad, Fool, Pool

My dad is such a fool
As he fell into the pool
Mum heard a great crack
Then she gave him a great whack
For playing the silly fool.

Molly Small (7)
Hammond School

The Light And Dark

Cats, dogs
Light, dark
Black, white
The opposites.
Lots of mops that will wash you away
Dancing, writing, lots of things
These are the things that will make your voice ring
Teachers or children,
Make you freak
When they say . . .
The light and the dark.

These shades are like a piano
With ebony and ivory keys.
If you see a volcano,
You'll see what I see!
The erupting, the shaking is different
But then you see a bee!
Tears, laughing is OK
But the dark isn't,
It is bad, mean, unthoughtful and unkind,
But the light is shiny, honest and is kind.
So this is the difference between . . .
The light and the dark.

Sarah Garmston (10)
Hammond School

I Once Saw A Huphalump

I once saw a huphalump
Sitting in a tree, I heard it singing,
'You can't catch me!'

I once saw a huphalump
Swimming in a pool, I heard it singing,
'You can't catch me!'

I once saw a huphalump
Sitting on the floor,
I thought it was dreaming
But must of guessed wrong
I then heard it singing,
'You can't catch me!'

I once saw a huphalump
Lying on the floor,
I thought it was going to say
You can't catch me, but I was wrong,
It said,
'Zzzzzzzzzzz.'
Shoosh it is asleep.

Holly Tarling (9)
Hammond School

January

The days are short,
The sun a spark,
Fat snowy footsteps
Track the floor
Milk bottles burst outside the door.

The river is a frozen place
Held beneath the trees of lace
The sky is low
The wind is grey
The radiator,
Purrs all day.

Gemma Horner (11)
Hammond School

Bonfire Night

See the Catherine wheels spinning through the dark
See the lights shining from the children's light sticks.
See the beautiful colours from the fireworks.
See the names made from the sparklers.

Hear the noise coming from the fireworks.
Hear the amazement from the crowd.
Hear the children screaming because of the fireworks.
Hear the Mums saying 'Don't be scared.'

Smell the ash from the bonfire.
Smell the burgers being cooked.
Smell the sausages sizzling.

Taste the marshmallows slowly melting in your mouth.
Taste the smoke when you breathe in.

Feel the heat on your face.

Emily Smith (8)
Hammond School

I Wish

I wish I knew, I wish I could,
Walk around my neighbourhood.
Underneath the sky is grey,
Graffiti sprayers in early day.
Please help us in this estate,
People playing out very late.
Scared and frightened without a sound,
Knowing horrible people are around.
Cars outside burnt and black,
Broken glass put in a sack.
They all got caught, graffiti painted,
Mum heard the good news and suddenly fainted.
Now I live in a peaceful, green place,
Now everyone has a happy face.

Lucy Thorpe (11)
Hammond School

Angry

Is a fierce feeling like a hairy baboon
bursting out of the treetops
to reach the light.
It is breaking me apart.
It is like a hideous snake
with poisoned fangs.
It is red like fire burning furiously.
It tastes like rotten blood.
It smells of dead bodies rotting.
It feels as if I'm blowing up.
It is ripping through me like a powerful
lion tearing the flesh off a gazelle.

Angry.

Liban (10)
Purley Oaks Primary School

Anger

It's an evil feeling
It's like a lioness or a vampire
that chases and bites the neck
of its prey.
I see red for I'm thirsty.
I'm very thirsty for blood.
it's like ripping the heart of someone.
Taking it, squeezing it in your hand.
It tastes like water and smells like fire.
It feels unnatural and evil.
It sounds like the roar of a lion.
it is indestructible.

Anger.

Mark Akiwumi (11)
Purley Oaks Primary School

Busted

Busted are cool.
Busted are the best.
Busted rock they do.
Busted are wicked.
Busted can rap.
Busted are good.
Busted are not bad!
Busted are stars.

Melissa Miah (9)
Purley Oaks Primary School

Calm

Calm is a peaceful feeling
Like water slowly raining over stones.
It's blue and like a dog cuddling up on your lap.
It is like everything is in slow motion.
It tastes like biscuits being dipped in tea.
It smells like someone baking scrumptious cakes.
It feels as if you could just lay down and go straight to sleep.
It is a relaxing feeling.
Calm.

Robert McQueen (10)
Purley Oaks Primary School

Embarrassed

Is a horrible feeling
Like a broken stone
It is hilarious for others
It tastes like an onion
It sounds like people
Laughing in the background
It feels as if it is flying around
Embarrassed.

Natasha Wilson (11)
Purley Oaks Primary School

Too Hard

As I stumbled in the awful stinky factory
I could smell the oil it smelt worse than stale cheese.
I felt like I was going to puke,
I just stopped myself.
The boss was walking towards me, I hid behind a machine.
He found me,
I ran for my life, I tripped over a rat
I really hurt my knee.
The boss picked me up by my ear
Argh!
The man whipped me
I screamed even louder.
'Shut up!' he shouted.
I went back to work.

Jake Sherafatmand (9)
Purley Oaks Primary School

Syndi The Cat

Syndi was a cat
Syndi was fat
Syndi was bloated
In white she was coated.

She listened to rock,
And the tick of the clock,
But one very special day,
Syndi went away.

She went to the road
She was chasing a toad,
Syndi was fat,
But Syndi went *splat!*

Ben Elliott (9)
Purley Oaks Primary School

The ABC Poem

A is for Annalise who picks her nose
B is for Ben who sucks his toes
C is for Chelsi who always gets into trouble
D is for Dyonne who's seeing double.
E is for Elle who's always watching TV.
F is for Farida who's scared of ET.
G is for Gemma who doesn't like the weather.
H is for Holly who's soft as a feather.
I is for Ivy, who likes to eat flies.
J is for Jessica who floats in the sky.
K is for Krassi who spends hours in the bath.
L is for Lucy who likes to have a laugh.
M is for Mary who likes to eat ice.
N is for Nathan who always lies.
O is for Oliver who is a cat.
P is for Page who poohed on the mat.
Q is for Queen who spent all her money.
R is for Ruby who doesn't like honey.
S is for Sam who doesn't like ham.
T is for Tegan who really likes jam.
U is for Unise who likes to fart.
V is for Vedna who likes to play darts.
W is for William who always wins the million.
X is for X-iyou who beats the billion.
Y is for Yasmin who's always bossy.
Z is for Zahrah who's always fussy.

Amina Matin (10)
Purley Oaks Primary School

Nan Can You Rap?

She rapped to the kitchen to get a cup of tea
Then she rapped to the toilet 'cause she needed a wee.

She rapped past the fish tank
And she rapped past the cake
Then when she turned the corner
She got bit by a snake

Then she rapped past Norway
And she rapped past Japan,
She rapped past a woman
And she rapped past a man.
'I'm the best rapping Gran this world's ever seen
I'm a zing zang tiny ting rap queen.'

She rapped past the seaweed
And she rapped past the clam.
She rapped past the lobster
And she rapped past Sam.

She rapped to the supermarket,
To buy a tin of beans.
'I'm the best rapping Gran this world's ever seen.
I'm a tic tac rig-raf rap rap
         Queen.'

Samuel Passman & Nathan Shaw (10)
Purley Oaks Primary School

I Saw . . .

I saw a snake with glittering scales
eat a rhino with a sharp horn.
I saw a giraffe doing the splits
in the wild.
I saw a Mummy suck the son's brains out.
I saw a bookshelf come to life and read a book.
I saw a mouse get ten metres long by the minute.
I saw a peacock talking to a bee.

Charlie Ell (8)
Purley Oaks Primary School

Skeleton

My freaky skeleton is white
He loves Hallowe'en
He loves to go to London Dungeons
He loves the cold
He wears a see-through blanket
He sits on a bony bench
He gets filmed on Scooby-Doo
He eats slimy worms.

Hannah Louise MacDonald (10)
Purley Oaks Primary School

Machine Poem

There I was crouching around the machines
Frightened as a frog.
It made me sneeze
Nobody was talking
It was like they had been put under a spell
The smell was awful
It smelled of rotten fish
But the workers were out of shape
Machines about to blow
The boss I saw
The man with a whip
I was terrified
The man I saw was very ugly and fat
He was stamping his posh shoes along the floor
Stepping towards me
About to whip me
All the workers got petrified
A baby was crying because of the smell of rotten fish
The machines were fearless
Like they were going to devour me.

Frankie Wigger (10)
Purley Oaks Primary School

Victorians Factory

Walking around the dark smelly machines
Terrified!
The workers were skinny like a skeleton
And were dirty.
I felt I was trapped in Hell.
I couldn't stop coughing
Because of the smell of oil.
I walked as slow and quiet
As possible so they didn't hear or see me.
It was loud like black thunder.
Then there were footsteps
It was the powerful boss with a whip.

Jessica Clarke (9)
Purley Oaks Primary School

Hell Factory

I crawled around the machines
Nearly got chopped
Very dark could not see a thing
Rats scurrying on the floorboards
Noises like Hell banging and smashing
Smelt like oil and polluted air
I felt like creeping out without being noticed
Felt like I was going to die
Workers looked so skinny I could see their
Bones they looked like ghosts!
The movement of the machines looked like
They were going to kill me.

Alicia Hall (9)
Purley Oaks Primary School

The Factory From Hell

It was dark, too dark,
Darker than black, it was
Pitch-black.
The machines were on but
No sound came out.
It was as if they were on mute.
I was terrified
There was no air or light.
It was hard to breathe.
It was warm,
The heaters were hot.
It smelt gruesome
Like oil and rats, tat, tat.
Boom, boom.
The lights came on
The women moaning and groaning
I hid away
It was terrifying.

Jordan Giddings (10)
Purley Oaks Primary School

My Fish

My fish is white and pink
She is a warm autumn
She is the inside of a fish bowl that is so sweet
She is a tropical fish that is multicoloured
She is a rough snake skin
She eats her own droppings
And her favourite film is Finding Nemo.

Nadereh Alvani (10)
Purley Oaks Primary School

Deadly

Is a dismal feeling
It feels like I am going bright red
It feels like a crocodile snapping
It is like a hurricane spinning me round and round
It tastes like a flame
It smells like the oven will blow up
It feels like lightning a tree
It is like hailstones dropping and scarring my face
Angry.

Peter Theobald (10)
Purley Oaks Primary School

The Frightening Factory

All alone!
The darkness is darker than I
Ever knew it could be.
The machines are roaring,
The whips are cracking,
I feel like I'm in Hell
I'm terrified.
This place is so smelly,
The smell smells like cow dung.
I feel like my life is fading away.
I feel like a prisoner, a slave.
The whip is coming, coming at me.
Crack. 'Yow' I screamed.
I hate this place.

Phillip Crawley (10)
Purley Oaks Primary School

Anger

Is a deathly feeling
It's like a guilty murderer
It's the colour of blood-red
Dripping down a table.
It tastes like dog hair stuck in the mouth.
It smells of a gone-off sandwich.
It feels as if you are a ferocious knife
Stabbing into something.
It's one experience you don't want.

Tinisha Ashley (11)
Purley Oaks Primary School

The Broken Silence

There I was . . .
All alone . . .
Lightning.
Thunder.
Storms, overpowering the air!
A trickle of fear shivered down my spine.
Darkness consuming the light.
The sun sank into the sea . . .
The moon took over.
It was dark . . . like Hell but worse!
It was too dark for my liking.
A flash of light . . . a crash and a shadow
Coming closer, closer, closer.
Then *bang!*
It was too late . . . madness had taken over . . .
Machines waiting to devour me
It was the end.

Nathaniel Bradshaw (10)
Purley Oaks Primary School

Too Late

I put my foot on the first step
Already I hear the machines screeching
I heard someone scream.
I could smell oil.
I poked my head round the wall
I could see machines
And a man
With a whip
It was bitterly cold
The machines look like they were ready to
Pounce like a dog does.
It made me feel sick
But it was too late to turn back.

Paige Griffiths (9)
Purley Oaks Primary School

The Dark Scary Factory

I tiptoed into the smelly factory.
I could hear people moaning about
Death!
I could hear the machines so loudly
It was like they were going to
Chop you up or
Explode!
It was so smelly I was almost
Sick . . .
Then I heard someone get whipped
For
Talking.
The children and adults were
So skinny
It was like they were
Trapped in a
Prison!

Zahrah Shah (9)
Purley Oaks Primary School

Hell Factory

Stepping foot in that factory
I smelt oil.
Crept past the machines
Tilting
Machines sounding as if they were going
to eat you.
Scared.
It was dark as the sky at night but worse
I was terrified.
I went to ask what am I to do?
Lowering down
Scared as a spider.
No one was talking I asked why.
'Shhh,' they said.
Boss saw me talk, all I felt was . . .
Clobber, 'Owww'
'Now get on.'

Danielle Clayden (10)
Purley Oaks Primary School

I Saw

I saw a leopard with pink and purple fur
I saw a green cat purr
I saw an orange person push a pram
I saw a person walk into a talking tram
I saw a house munch the moon
I saw a plate gobble up a spoon
I saw a bottle drink some water
I saw my mum eat someone's daughter.

Rosie McGarry (8)
Purley Oaks Primary School

Nonsense

What is nonsense I ask?
Is it where dogs moo
And pigs fly?
What is nonsense I ask?
Is it where ponies go 'Give me all your money?'
Is it where shoplifters tell the truth?
What is nonsense I ask?
Is it where pigs put lipstick on
And girls have short hair?

　　What is nonsense?

Aaliyah Binnie (8)
Purley Oaks Primary School

The Factory

Darkness consumed me.
I was drowning in an everlasting pit of black.
Over the roar of the machines, the crack of a whip.
Argh!
Crying, muffled by the machines, filled my ears.
Puddles of oil on the floor.
The smell's gut-rotting and sickening.
My legs went numb.
Whip!
Screams rang throughout my ears and head.
Creak!
The door opened.
Light poured in.
Figures.
Figures coming towards me.
Figures of people, stick people.
Stick people with limp hair, lifeless faces
And bones for bodies.
Whispers . . .

Harriet Fiddimore (9)
Purley Oaks Primary School

The Horrible Factory

I tiptoed inside shivering,
It was dark and cold
I was worried and frightened
It was like I had just fallen in a
Coffin!

The machines were loud,
They looked like giant crushers about to
Kill me!

I thought if I stepped one step further
I would smell horrible old air,
Forever in a horrible dark factory.

I walked shivering forward
I didn't want to, but I had to,
The boss was stomping around,
Then!
He stomped towards me
Big cross face with cane in his hand,
Then
Bang!
He whipped me.

Emma Hallett (9)
Purley Oaks Primary School

Sad

Sad is a cheerless feeling,
Like a child with no friends.
It's blue like a jailed man in an electric chair.
It is grim and pitiful.
It tastes of salt.
It smells wet and musky.
It feels as if I'm the only person on Earth.
Sad.

Hannah Clarke (11)
Purley Oaks Primary School

Anger

Anger
Is a livid feeling
It is red like blood when you've cut yourself
It is horrid like a haunted house
It tastes like burnt cookies on a cold winter's night
It smells like bad breath from a drunk teenager
It feels as if your brain is about to explode
It is sour like a lemon from the fridge
Anger.

Adam Hill (11)
Purley Oaks Primary School

The Storm

The lightning's flashing
The forest is crashing
A man called to me
Said it soon will be gone.

But now nobody fears
As the dreadful storm clears
All the winds passing by
As the bright sun comes by.

But when it comes back
The people hack.

But now it's gone by
The people cry.

But when the storm
Comes back
The trees all crack
As it comes by the babies cry.

Now it's all gone
We all are fond
We all come out
No storm about.

Joshua Steventon (9)
Purley Oaks Primary School

It Makes Me Really Angry

It makes me really angry
When I can't go out to play
I look at the drops of rain
I do it every day.

It makes me really angry
When I can't go to sleep
What's that racket down there
The tune goes beep, beep.

It makes me really angry
Can I watch TV?
Oh I can't again
Why is it always me?

It makes me really angry
When I have to have my shower
This time I sneezed
Because I found a flower.

Jenna Ram (8)
Purley Oaks Primary School

I Saw

I saw a mouse flying in the sky
I saw a white shark fly in the air
I saw Luke being bossy
I saw a girl lay an egg
I saw a dog dancing
I saw China get demolished
I saw a person flying
I saw a baby chop off a huge tree
I saw Robbie (who is in EastEnders) at the big pantomime.

Daanish Shahid (8)
Purley Oaks Primary School

Life In A Victorian Factory

I shivered inside
It was dark like Hell
It felt creepy and lonely
No one was talking
The machines were loud
The people looked skinny, dirty
And their bones were showing
It smelled oily and of smoke
It was loud like black thunder
Terrifying whip
Horrifying *scream.*

Ling Tang (9)
Purley Oaks Primary School

The Factory

Crouching past huge black crushing machines
Terrified of the machines
It was so dark I could not see my hands
Some workers were so skinny, I could see their skeletons
One of the old men whispered to himself
Five more years
It's so loud like a stampede of elephants
I could smell the oil, it stank.
I feel terrified of everything
Arrgh poor boy three times today he's been
Whipped.
If I had the power
I would teach him
I just have to put up with him
I better go crouch around
I don't want to get in trouble
I better work hard.

Joseph Blackwood (10)
Purley Oaks Primary School

Straight Out Of Hell

There I was,
Those skeletons working as if they wanted to eat me.
Bang!
Gone, slipped away into the darkness.
All alone.
Like a plague of darkness had swept over me.
I felt cold.
I felt lonely.
They're back!
I start to work.
I could see the boss with a concave stick.
I pull that thing up and down.
Couldn't control it!
Argh!
She wasn't moving
The machine's still tilting
Here's the end.

Jacob Vibetti (10)
Purley Oaks Primary School

The Animal Poem

A jumping dolphin
A big grey shark
A smelly pig on the farm
A mouse smelling cheese
A fish swimming away
A giraffe eating leaves from the trees
A leopard running for its prey
A parrot chatting, chatting away.

Robyn Payne (8)
Purley Oaks Primary School

Hell On Earth

I was just entering the factory
So quiet they're so skinny like skeletons
I was creaking around
People just working
No sound at all
It was dark black
With no lights at all
It looked like Hell come down
To Earth
There were slaves
People got whipped for talking
It made me scared
I was so poorly and ill and nearly lifeless
I felt like screaming inside
I feel like a slave
There were many different jobs
Banging and chopping anything you can imagine
workers just sweating away.

Rebecca Harvey (10)
Purley Oaks Primary School

The Creepy Factory

There was something creeping around the factory.
It was thumping
Really loud.
It was the headman.
Horrible!
You would not want to see him on a dark night.
The machines were so loud
The machines have taken over the world.

Louis Brixey (10)
Purley Oaks Primary School

I Wish

I wish a jungle full of animals.
Pleasant ones.
Some kind, gentle, soft,
Some with wings, some with not,
Some a bit grumpy,
Some will sting,
Some with hairy legs,
Some who are cuddly.

I wish I had some animals
Like lions but friendly ones,
Beautiful butterflies,
Baby tigers,
Fluffy cuddly bears,
Insects,
Elephants and a monkey.

Joanne Matheson (9)
Purley Oaks Primary School

Animals

In a zoo there are

A nimals from near and far like
N oisy parrots who squawk
I nsects in glass cages
M onkeys swinging from every tree
A lligators snapping their big jaws
L azy lions sitting in the sun
S illy seals balancing balls on their heads.

Jessica Field (8)
Purley Oaks Primary School

All Alone

On my own,
Small, overpowered
Grinding teeth of the machines
Ready to pounce.
It was dark
Worse
It was like the end of the world
Silence
As if my mind was dead
A skeleton! A fellow worker
My eyes darted from place to place
My teeth chattered in my mouth
They wanted to get out
Crack! A whip
The shriek of a worker
I wanted to scream
I wanted to run
I couldn't.

Georgia Kelly (10)
Purley Oaks Primary School

Anger

Is a deadly feeling
Like boiling water spilling on the floor
It is red like blood splattered around a crime scene
It is like a dagger embedded in someone
It tastes of burnt toast
It smells like overcooked eggs
It feels as if you are covered in molten lava.
It is falling off a diving board.

Anger.

Ken Robertson (10)
Purley Oaks Primary School

Aggressive

Aggressive
Is a violent feeling
Like a huge storm
It is a green sky ready to toss hailstones
It is punching with its stone fists
It tastes like rotten eggs
It smells like smoke from fire
It feels as if you are being kicked
It is a hurricane spinning everything around
Aggressive.

Vikki-Louise Parker (11)
Purley Oaks Primary School

Anger

Anger
Is a raving feeling
Like some boiled eggs frying in a pan
It is as red as a tomato
It is an enraged and grumpy feeling you don't want to have
It tastes like burnt toast
It smells like a burning fire
It feels as if you're a different person
It is a disease fuming wrathful
Anger.

Carl Shephard (11)
Purley Oaks Primary School

I Sit Here On The Train

I sit here on the train,
Wondering what lies ahead
Thinking about my wife
My wife that will not have me by her side
When my child is born
What is going on in Hitler's mind?
What is telling him to do this?
What good does he think will come of this?
Is he crazy? Yes, he must be.
I sit here on the train
Thinking of this.
While the other soldiers play cards and talk
But I sit alone, thinking of my wife
And of my brothers and sisters,
Who came to see big brother go,
And kill 'nasty Hitler men.'
I sit here on the train
Wondering if I'll see them again
Hug them close and hold them tight.
I sit here on the train
Alone, thinking, wondering.

Katie Elliott (11)
Purley Oaks Primary School

Animal Poem

The fast cheetah pounces on its prey
A starfish floats in the sea
One stripy tall zebra runs for its prey
A small prickly hedgehog curls into a ball
The spotty long giraffe stretches its long neck
And eats some leaves.
A small soft mouse crawls to eat some grass.

Darcie Kelly (9)
Purley Oaks Primary School

Sound Poem

Now is the time of night, I can hear . . .
A train rushing past like a herd of elephants
racing for life.

Now is the time of night, I can hear . . .
Next door singing really loudly as if
the radio's too loud.

Now is the time of night I can hear . . .
My mum turning on the TV looking for
something good to watch.

Now is the time of day I can hear . . .
The birds singing a soft tune like a flute.

Yasmeen Hussain (9)
Purley Oaks Primary School

The Silly Poem!

Animals are blue
Jelly beans are glue
Televisions laugh
Dolls take a bath
Lamps dance around
On the big fat ground
Shoes go on your head
And bags go to bed.

Tahnée Seagrave (8)
Purley Oaks Primary School

Town And Country

Look at the country the animals are asleep.
Look at the city busy as can be.
Look at the country, it is so delightful and relaxed.
Look at the crowded city, it is so dirty and polluted.
Look at the country it is so graceful and calm as can be.
Look at the noisy city, it is so deafening and hectic.
Look at the country, it is so quiet and peaceful.
Look at the city it is so interesting and exciting.
Look at the country it is so tranquill and beautiful.

Nicola Rogers (8)
Purley Oaks Primary School

Becky's Pets

In Becky's cellar she kept. . .
Ten red big fat chickens
Nine big eyed running snakes
Eight cats running up the stairs
Seven flying white birds
Six big brown dogs
Five flies dancing around
Four big crawling worms
Three mooing cows mooing
Two white mice
And one. . . guess what it is?

Nazifa Hossain (8)
Purley Oaks Primary School

Afraid

Afraid
Is an uneasy feeling
Like a horrified ant about to be stepped on
It is blue like a person being washed out to sea
It is frightened of everything it does
It tastes of your worst taste, like mushrooms
It smells of nervous sweat
It feels as if you're scared when you have to read out
It is faint-hearted,
Afraid.

Tiana Hutton (11)
Purley Oaks Primary School

Furious

Is an angry feeling
Like red blood falling from Hell.
It's red and black colours of evilness
There is no escape from fury
It tastes like sick in your throat
It smells like garbage being tossed at you
It feels like fire is burning everywhere
Fire is in your eyes
It is fury.

Lauren Ward (10)
Purley Oaks Primary School

Peaceful

Peacefulness
Is a calming feeling
Like fish swimming in and out of seaweed
It is all pastel colours like a pencil pack
It is a slow, serene feeling like rippling water
It tastes of ice cream melting in your tummy
It smells like flowers in a meadow in spring
It feels as if you're surrounded by soft teddies
And you're falling asleep
It reminds you of rabbits and deer playing in a forest
It's a feeling you want to be part of.

    Peaceful.

Jessica Buswell (11)
Purley Oaks Primary School

Lonely

Lonely is a friendless feeling
Like a tree in the desert on his own
It is quiet
It tastes of grass
It smells of sand
It feels like you are upset
It is single
Lonely.

Kirstie Rogers (11)
Purley Oaks Primary School

The Football That Left No Sound
(Based on 'The Sound Collector' by Roger McGough)

A stranger came to a football match
In a nice Ferrari car
I put all the sounds into a bag
And ran away so far.

The kicking of the ball
The screaming of the crowd
When you score a goal
It starts to get quite loud.

The clacking of the rattlers
The chatting of the fans
The *woohhh* that people make
When it hits the goalie's hands.

A stranger came to a football match
He didn't leave his name
Left us only silence
Life will never be the same.

Callum McGerly, Alex Hill (9) & Charlie Kimber (10)
Purley Oaks Primary School

Puppy

My puppy is brown
She is autumn
Wrapped in a blanket
She wears a gown of
Slinky silk leaves.
She likes it when it's windy
She lies in a basket
Watching Scooby-Doo
Whilst chewing a juicy bone.

Abigail Mullins (11)
Purley Oaks Primary School

The Romans

All of the Romans fight, fight, fight
They live with their families when they sleep at night
In the morning children play,
While some parents watch not far away.
If you are an Emperor that's fine,
Sit and relax as you drink a glass of fresh wine,
Times are different now,
Just think how!
For us we sit at home,
But think what it was like back in mystical Rome.

Kaitlyn Sheeran (9)
Purley Oaks Primary School

The Countryside

Look at the countryside it is so quiet.
It is so peaceful.
It is so beautiful and fresh.
The countryside is full of trees.
The countryside is full of wonderful animals.
There are wonderful clean ponds in the countryside.
There are lovely green hills.
There are white fluffy sheep on the farms.

Gurpreet Ubi (8)
Purley Oaks Primary School

The Countryside And City Poem

The countryside is quiet and calm
The city is loud with people in harm.
The countryside has lots of oxen
The city has lots of foxes.
The countryside has lots of sheep
The city has lots of cars that go beep.

Charlotte Hedley (8)
Purley Oaks Primary School

Happy

Happy is the feeling of floating on the cloud.
Happy is the feeling of happy faces.
Happy is the feeling of making friends.
Happy is the feeling of butter melting in your mouth.
Happy is the feeling of funny monkeys dancing.
Happy is the feeling of the lovely smell of lavender.
Happy is the feeling of lovely smell of the daisy flowers.
Happy is the feeling of the lovely wet sound of the water statues.
Happy is the feeling of the lovely bright colours.
Happy is the feeling of dancing in the moonlight.

Kainat Syeda (8)
Purley Oaks Primary School

Town

The town is crowded
The town is polluted
The town is loud
The town is busy
The town is dirty
The town is dusty
The town is smoky
The town is smelly
The town is dark
The town is bright.

Kelsey Stracey (9)
Purley Oaks Primary School

I Saw

I saw a balloon wider than the moon
I saw the sun set brighter than the moon
I saw an ant carrying the house
I saw a bell quieter than a mouse
I saw some white prickly rice
I saw a big lump of frostbiting ice
I saw a different coloured snake
I saw a wavy sort of lake
I saw a mermaid green and pink
I saw the teacher using unusual ink
I saw a man eating some roast chicken
I saw a woman eating in the kitchen.

Lenina Aung-Mya (9)
Purley Oaks Primary School

The Busy City

The roads are busy,
The buildings are too.
A pity that,
Planes are landing,
Buses are stopping,
People are running,
The sun is rising,
The clouds are black,
The people are sweating
And the water is cold.

Joel Livesley (8)
Purley Oaks Primary School

I Saw

I saw a fairy
with short pink wings.
I saw her sitting on a rock
jingling her rings.
No you never, you never
I did.

I saw a tiger
open his mighty mouth.
I saw him creeping
towards the south.
No you never, you never
I did.

I saw a monster
with hairy toes
I saw the monster
picking his nose.
No you never, you never
I did.

I saw your mum
going through your phone book.
I saw your mum take the phone off the hook.
No you never, you never
You did!

Lola Meredith (9)
Purley Oaks Primary School

Humpty Dumpty

Humpty Dumpty, he was not hurt
Humpty Dumpty was covered in dirt
All the queen's horses and all the king's knights
Had to get Humpty and put him in tights.

Humpty Dumpty ran down a hill
Humpty Dumpty fell very ill
All the king's horses and all the king's knights
Opened Humpty's mouth and switched on his lights.

Chris Carr (9)
St Anne's RC Primary School, Banstead

Humpty Dumpty

Humpty Dumpty went to a school
Humpty Dumpty sat in a hall
He went on a school trip
To London zoo
And there he shook hands
With a kangaroo.

John O'Connor (8)
St Anne's RC Primary School, Banstead

Humpty Dumpty

Humpty Dumpty had a small sleep,
Humpty Dumpty started to weep.
When he woke up, he felt very sad,
Along came his friend and made him feel glad.

Katie Foster (7)
St Anne's RC Primary School, Banstead

Humpty Dumpty

Humpty Dumpty went to a hall
Humpty Dumpty went to a ball
Humpty Dumpty was a very, very good boy
And he was famous for being a toy.

The next day Humpty went to the zoo
He said, 'Wait, I need to tie up my shoe'
All the zoo animals and all the zookeepers
Didn't eat Humpty because they weren't very good eaters.

Niamh Carr (7)
St Anne's RC Primary School, Banstead

Humpty Dumpty

Humpty Dumpty felt very ill
Humpty Dumpty rang Uncle Bill
Humpty Dumpty had a hot cup of tea
Humpty Dumpty swallowed a chimpanzee.

Steven McNally
St Anne's RC Primary School, Banstead

Humpty Dumpty

Humpty Dumpty was very cool
Humpty Dumpty played with a ball
All of his fun friends were really jazzy,
Wore lovely clothes that were very snazzy.

Emma Neil-Jones (8)
St Anne's RC Primary School, Banstead

Jack And Jill

Jack and Jill
Went to football
To see their uncle playing,
Jack dived down
And went to town
And they both started praying.

Clare Conway (8)
St Anne's RC Primary School, Banstead

Humpty Dumpty

Humpty Dumpty went to the zoo
Humpty Dumpty needed the loo
All the zookeepers and all the zoo men
They wanted Humpty to fetch a gold hen.

Louis Clarke (7)
St Anne's RC Primary School, Banstead

Jack And Jill

Jack and Jill
Were very ill,
They went to bed
With their ted.

They went down
And gave a frown
Because their mum
Made some bread.

Georgie Hobern (8)
St Anne's RC Primary School, Banstead

I See A Snowflake

I see a snowflake
Gently falling
Twisting and turning
As white as snow like a star
Softly silent
Settling on the pavement
Sadly melting.

I see an icicle
Freezing carefully
Still and frozen
Like a ghost
Ice cream cone
Crackling sharply
Sadly drips away.

Fern Thomas (8)
St Luke's Primary School, Kingston

Fireworks

Frightened cat cuddles cosily
Warm and safe under the bed
Away from loud banging fireworks.
Cat is lonely and afraid.
Cat sitting near fire warm
Curled in a ball cosy
Watch the fireworks from kitchen windows.
Cat scared, angry.
Fireworks bang really loud and make your ears pop
Fireworks night is really important to me
Because it is a big night and it's nice.
My mum made some jokes about the fireworks.

Anna-Marie Lloyd (9)
St Luke's Primary School, Kingston

Fire

The dancing flames
The scalding heat
The blazing colour
The crackling sound

The misty smoke
The vanishing wood
The jet-black coal
The patterned frame

The dangerous chances
That you could get burnt
That you could vanish
Into flames

Any guesses
I bet you know now
The one thing that can burn you
Fire.

Jenny Irving (8)
St Luke's Primary School, Kingston

Firework Night

Fantastic swirl
Wonderful shine
Catherine wheels spin
Fire flickers
Sparklers wave about
Making patterns in the dark
Explosions of colour in the sky
When you think it's all over
Another one goes up
Bang! Crack! Sizzle!
Fire fades away
People leave
Flames blow away in the night sky.

Ruby Mae Gibbs (8)
St Luke's Primary School, Kingston

The Swan

Wings moving so swiftly,
Body moving so slow,
Swooping down peacefully,
Gliding down so low.

Flying around so carefully,
Very brave and strong,
Talented, while flying gracefully,
Elegant movement, body so long.

Positive about where he's going,
Body as white as snow,
Intelligent, tantalizing,
Where he's meant to go.

Getting faster by the minute,
Gruncher just right there,
Human right in front of him,
Something he just can't bear.

Nearly, nearly by the lake,
Gruncher close behind,
In he goes into our wake,
Nothing left to remind us.

Katie L Hughes (8)
St Luke's Primary School, Kingston

I See A Snowflake

I see a snowflake,
A snowflake falling from the sky,
Floating like a cloud,
Its colour is white.
Snowflake is shaped round,
Like a circle.
The trees are covered with snow
And the logs are covered with ice.
Snowball is cold as an ice cube,
If you touch it your hand will freeze.

Sayed Adil Naziri (9)
St Luke's Primary School, Kingston

Beautiful Swan

Beautiful swan
So calm and careful
Strong and brave
White as snow
Tease, tease, tease

Graceful as ever
Peacefully swooping low
Gliding positively
Beauty it has
Glides, glides, glides

Calm and fearless
Swiftly, delicately
Talented and smooth
Elegant, intelligent
Willing, willing, willing.

Bella Horwood (9)
St Luke's Primary School, Kingston

The Confused Firework

Sparks fly off the confused firework.
It gets ready to fly.
It takes off.
It soars up into the sky.

Bang!

It explodes.
Now millions of colours appear in the air.
Now it's all stopped and the firework has gone.

Josh Harris (9)
St Luke's Primary School, Kingston

Bonfire Night

Hedgehog smells the burning,
Sees the light and hears the crackling,
Feels the warmth and can't resist.
Scuttles in, there's insects to eat.
Big bangs, beautiful music, sparkling colours.
Patters out of the bonfire
And stares at the spinning Catherine wheel instead.

Elinor Anghileri (9)
St Luke's Primary School, Kingston

Fireworks

Cosy cat, nice and warm
Curled up safe, hears the banging
Of the fireworks, wakes up,
No one there.
Creeps up to the window.
Back to his cosy bed, nice and warm.
Back to sleep,
No one is there to play with him.
All the colours that brighten up the sky.
The people, shouting,
The cat's alarmed at all the noise,
Can't go to sleep.
He is very safe after all.
He puts his paws over his ears.
He creeps up the stairs.
Cold and lonely, looks out of the window
At the fireworks.
He is afraid of the fireworks.
He ducks down as a rocket shoots.

Alice Foster (8)
St Luke's Primary School, Kingston

The Gala

I come ready for the gala
Costume and hat on
Goggles tight
Trembling with fright.

On the blocks
Ready to go
The beeper beeps
Dive down deep.

Suddenly I'm a dolphin
Flipping through the sea
Propelling myself forward.

I see the end
It's coming close
Cheers echo round the pool
I need more breath
I mustn't choke
I feel like I need a Coke.

I'm nearly there
Just about to touch
I hope I come first
But maybe
I might be second, or third, or fourth.

Last stroke
I come up gasping
Faces everywhere
Do I care?
I look around.

Did I win?

Amelia Brown (8)
St Luke's Primary School, Kingston

I Know It's Snowing

In the pitch-black nights
The painful frost bites.
With the cold winter wind blowing
I know it is snowing.

The tall standing trees
With no blowing leaves.
With the ground glowing
I know it is snowing.

A chilling breeze
Frost-covered leaves.
The howling winds not going
I know it is snowing,
Yes, I know it is snowing.

Ryan Wheeler (8)
St Luke's Primary School, Kingston

Kitty

Bang goes a firework up in the sky,
Kitty curls up all petrified.
Lonely and confused at what's going on,
Kitty hears singing of her favourite song.
Click goes the door latch, someone comes in,
Kitty feels a warm blow of the wind.
As the door is closing Kitty feels safe and cosy,
Kitty sees a glowing light coming near.
She starts to quiver.
The door clicks open once again,
Kitty hears lots of footsteps on the kitchen floor.
Kitty is now not so lonely.

Isabelle DuBois (8)
St Luke's Primary School, Kingston

Fireworks

Petrified cat safe inside
Cat lonely but cosy inside
Curled up like a little mouse
Not a sound at all
Just a little spark in the air
There he goes.

Henna Khan (8)
St Luke's Primary School, Kingston

Happiness Is . . .

Happiness is the sound of spring,
Life reappearing, starlings sing.

Happiness is the summer breeze,
Animals hunt their food with ease.

Happiness is the autumn air,
Wonderful colours for us to share.

Happiness is winter's song,
It won't be lasting for very long.

Jessica Dunne (9)
St Luke's Primary School, Kingston

Monday's Child

Monday's child has lost a tooth,
Tuesday's child has climbed up on the roof,
Wednesday's child has got no hair,
Thursday's child is eating a pear,
Friday's child has broken an arm,
Saturday's child has gone to visit a farm,
And the child that's born on Sunday,
Is all lonely, with no one to play.

Elena Somovilla (10)
St Peter's Primary School, South Croydon

Back To School

Back to school
Open new book
Write with new pen
Play with friends
Two weeks later
I'm bored
I'm ill
I don't like you
That's mine!
Six weeks gone
Phew, Christmas holiday!
Wow! I got this
What did you get?
I got that
You stole that!
That's mine!
Three weeks later
Nine fights
Two black eyes
And broken thumb
Half-term
Sunbathing
Holiday going
Having fun
What did you do?
I did nothing
I cleaned my bedroom
But all you've done to me all term
Is bother me!

Trainette Gillam (9)
St Peter's Primary School, South Croydon

Where Are The Handwriting Pens?

Come into the staffroom,
Written on the board,
'Where are the handwriting pens?'
Well . . . the room goes quiet.
'I took two for my classroom,' says Mrs Sandle,
'And I took ten for my classroom,' says Mrs Warde.
'Well, where are the others then?
I though we ordered 20, not 12!'
'Oh yes, I just remembered, the delivery man could not bring
any more than 12,' said Mrs Harris.
'Oh well, at least we have found that out!'

Emma Penn (9)
St Peter's Primary School, South Croydon

Polluted Streets

I am a street that's supposed to be neat,
Instead I am cluttered with things people eat.
I am a street, sticky with chewing gum,
On me people go and new people come.
On a pavement that is new,
With chewing gum stuck to people's shoes.

I am a street that's supposed to look good,
I would keep myself clean if only I could.
Covered with rubbish
And chips and fish,
People dragging shoelaces,
So streets have dirty faces.

Louise Fallon (9)
St Peter's Primary School, South Croydon

The Lost Paintbrush

One Friday afternoon, we'd just finished art,
Literacy was on the board, we were ready to start.
Mrs Crunchball counted the paintbrushes,
There was one missing.
'No one's going home until we find the missing paintbrush.'
Children looked under tables and chair,
They could not find the paintbrush anywhere!
At last we found the paintbrush, it was stuck in glue,
But still it looked brand new.
At last we managed to break it free,
All thanks to Mrs Honeybee!

Cherise Goode (10)
St Peter's Primary School, South Croydon

The Biscuit Tin

I hid the biscuit tin.
'Where is the biscuit tin?' Mum said.
'I don't know,' I said.
'Where is the biscuit tin?' said Dad.
'I don't know,' I said.
'Where are the biscuits?' said Josh.
'I don't know,' I said.
I lost the biscuit tin.
'You've got the biscuit tin,' said everyone.
'No I haven't.'
'Yes you have.'
'No I haven't, not anymore.'
'*Oh no!*'
'Oh yes, I hid them behind the door!'

Esther Mullins (10)
St Peter's Primary School, South Croydon

The Nightmare

I am in my bed
I rest my cold head
I wake up in the road
I am a bouncing toad
A car comes flashing by
Suddenly I eat a fly

I see my mum
She is drinking rum
She turns into a punk
She stamps on me
Suddenly I appear in a sea

I'm drowning
I'm frowning
I scream
I'm tearing at the seam
Of my PJs in my bed
I rest my head
I am awake.

Ruth Endersby (10)
St Peter's Primary School, South Croydon

Money!

Money, money, I love money
I love, I love, I love honey
Money, money, it makes you rich or poor
Money, money, everyone wants more and more
Money, money, it's everywhere, everybody does not care
Money, money, I spend more and more
Now I am getting very poor
Money, money, now I am coming to the end
Because I need to spend, spend, spend!

Chloé Rushton (9)
St Peter's Primary School, South Croydon

Teachers

There's a teacher who's always forgetful,
There's a teacher who's a singer,
There's a teacher who's always drinking her coffee in the morning.
There's a teacher who's always strict,
There's a teacher who does drama,
There's a teacher who's always smart,
There's another teacher who's a pianist,
There's a teacher who's a computer star
And there's a teacher who always does science.

Lauren Allam (9)
St Peter's Primary School, South Croydon

Ballet

Today I started ballet,
It was really, really scary,
We were practising for the show,
I was the fairy.

I didn't know what to wear,
So I wore my old black tights,
I didn't know what to bring
And they all had kites.

I also wore my fairy costume,
Which really fitted in,
I will do ballet forever and ever
And become very thin.

Laura Stone (9)
St Peter's Primary School, South Croydon

The Monster Under The Stairs

The monster under the stairs,
Everybody it scares.
It's extremely big,
But as slow as a pig,
And it's giving me nightmares!

The monster under the stairs,
It makes as much noise as it dares.
It woke me last night,
With an awful big fright,
And I don't think even Mum cares!

The monster under the stairs,
Out of its mouth come solar flares.
When I open the door,
It lets out a roar,
If not, it just sits there and glares!

The monster under the stairs,
It's got long, dirty hairs.
Always mad,
Never sad,
Oh, I'm sorry, it's Dad!

Samuel Taylor (9)
St Peter's Primary School, South Croydon

Chocolate

Chocolate, chocolate, I love chocolate,
It's so adorable,
Eating chocolate till I'm full,
So much chocolate I feel sick,
Get me to the toilet quick.

Chocolate is very yummy,
In my big fat tummy,
I like chocolate, what about you?
No, I don't, I'd rather eat a didgeridoo.

Poppy Nicholas (9)
St Peter's Primary School, South Croydon

The Spooky House

As I walk down the stairs, the stairs creak,
As I walk through a door, a mouse squeaks,
As I walk into the basement, bats fly around me,
As I turn on the tap, the fish sink to the bottom of the ocean,
As I get into bed, all is silent,
The lights flicker and now I'm frightened!

Ciara Coleman (9)
St Peter's Primary School, South Croydon

Can I Have . . . ?

An apple pie that is warm,
No bits, no crust, no parts that are torn,
A roller coaster in my backyard,
The biggest, the bestest, don't make it hard.

A day off school, yes that would be good,
Don't tell them you know I could,
A palace that's as big as the sun,
You know it's right, it can be done.

A massive chocolate and fudge cake,
Or even a mixture that I can bake,
An older brother with a motorbike,
Because I've only got a 3-wheel trike.

A best friend to help me in life,
I would try not to get into strife,
That's actually all I want for now,
Only one person to be my pal.

Jodie Pain (11)
St Peter's Primary School, South Croydon

There's A Monster Under My Bed

There's a monster under my bed
Sometimes I hope it's dead
I think it needs to be fed
There's a monster under my bed!

There's a monster under my bed
Sometimes I hope it's my teddy
I know her name is Betty
There's a monster under my bed.

There's a monster under my bed
I think it's a boy and his name is Freddy
Or maybe it's my uncle's teddy
There's a monster under my bed - *argh!*

Alexandra Nicholls (9)
St Peter's Primary School, South Croydon

Food

I like banana
I like cheese
I don't like yoghurt on my knees!

I like soup
I like stew
I don't like yoghurt on my shoe!

I like mango
I like bread
I don't like yoghurt on my head!

I like chocolate
I like sweets
I don't like yoghurt on my feet!

I like fish
I like chips
I don't like yoghurt anymore!

Jamie Askew (10)
St Peter's Primary School, South Croydon

Where Is The Chocolate Monster?

Where is the chocolate monster?
Under my big brother's bed
In the chocolate drawer,
Or maybe in the dark closet
Under the cupboard near the stairs,
Or maybe under the kitchen sink
Or outside in the garden,
Or maybe in the little shed,
Perhaps behind a picture.
But no one really knows.
Or perhaps it can be my sister's cute teddy bear.
My mum and dad get stressed
'Cause all the chocolates are gone.
But let me tell you something,
It's me!
And I'm hiding in the dishwasher.

Maria Christodoulides (10)
St Peter's Primary School, South Croydon

Haunted House

In the haunted house there is a scary ghost,
Everywhere you go you bump into an invisible post.
There's raw bones sat upon a plate,
Which vampires ate.
In the room next door there are bats,
As strong as wild cats.
In the haunted house it is as scary as that.

Joe Lobow (9)
St Peter's Primary School, South Croydon

Beast In The Bedroom

There's something in the bedroom
Scaring Mum and Dad
I don't know what it is
But it's making me mad!

There's something in the bedroom
Smashing all my things
I don't know what it is
But it's got huge feet and wings.

There's something in the bedroom
It's big and really hairy
I don't know what it is
But it's really, really scary!

There's something in the bedroom
I know what it is
I know what it's doing
It's scaring Auntie Liz!

Sarah Amrani (10)
St Peter's Primary School, South Croydon

The Day It Snows

It's snowing, it's snowing,
And the wind is strongly blowing,
Let's make a massive snowman
And keep it for as long as we can.

In this lovely snow,
You will never feel low,
The snow is as white as paper
And it melts as it gets later.

The snow will soon be gone,
It's not here for very long,
So make the most of it
And use every little bit.

Ariana Bravo (10)
St Peter's Primary School, South Croydon

Then I Decided . . .

My teacher said she was always good
My teacher said she never would
Tease her sister and make her cry
From the baker's steal a pie.

I asked her how she lived her life
Not getting caught in a strife
With her mum or dad
This story that I'm telling is really too bad.

I don't know if it's true
Could I really be like you
Never doing anything bad
    Not lying to my mum or dad?

Then I decided . . .

I'm not going to be good
Although I know I should
I'm not going to be bad
I'm just going to be flippin' mental and *mad!*

Kerry Goodwin (10)
St Peter's Primary School, South Croydon

Daydreams

I am flying on a piece of paper
And crashing into walls.
I am walking on my head
Round and round the sink.
I'm playing Quidditch
On a flying chair made of leaves.
I'm getting a drink
While I'm snowboarding on the table.
I'm jumping on a trampoline
And I freeze in the air.

Stanley Payne (7)
St Peter's Primary School, South Croydon

Daydream

Mrs Palmer thinks I'm reading,
But no, I've gone back in time,
I'm fighting Romans,
I'm playing football with the sun,
Ow! I burnt my foot.
Mrs Palmer thinks I'm drawing a boat,
But no, I am the boat,
I live in a cave,
I'm eating a slug-flavoured ice cream.
Mrs Palmer thinks I'm painting,
But no, I'm flying on a flying carpet,
I meet a witch and she casts a spell on me.
Dar, dar, dot, dot, leg of frog, nose of dog,
Turn her into a warthog.
Mrs Palmer thinks I'm working,
But no, I'm sailing the seven seas,
Splash! I fell in the water,
I sank down and down,
I have a fight with an octopus and a squid.

Madeleine Wilson (7)
St Peter's Primary School, South Croydon

Daydreams

Mrs Smithe thinks I'm working,
But I'm sitting on the ground.
Mrs Smithe thinks I'm reading,
But I'm pulling her ear in her eardrum.
Mrs Smithe thinks I'm painting,
But I'm licking the class.
Mrs Smithe thinks I'm listening,
But I'm puffing smoke out of my mouth.
Mrs Smithe thinks I'm running,
But I'm playing Chuckle Vision.
Mrs Smithe thinks I'm singing,
But I'm shining with glory.

Mazvita Msemburi (7)
St Peter's Primary School, South Croydon

The Poet

I don't know where to start,
Where do I begin?
A story full of happiness,
A story full of sin.
A knight in shining armour,
A maiden in distress,
A groom's top hat and coat,
A bridesmaid's silky dress.
Then in walks the bride,
All dressed in white,
She does look a sight,
Help! I need another line!
'You almost had a story there,
'Twas too good to be true,
Now our bride shall never marry
And it's all because of you!
Look beyond the obvious story,
There must be something there,
A handsome prince in exile,
A girl with golden hair.'

As you see, a story this was meant to be,
But instead a poem you got from me!
Don't make me write description,
Or think up a fantastic plot,
For this talent in poetry,
Is all that I have got.

Tamara Bazil (11)
St Peter's Primary School, South Croydon

I'm No Good At . . .

I'm no good at English
I'm no good at art
And when it comes to numeracy
You couldn't call me smart.

Don't tell me to write a story
'Cause I wouldn't even try
I'd come to you with rubbish
And I'll tell you the reason why.

Chorus:
I'm no good at English
I'm no good at art
And when it comes to numeracy
You couldn't call me smart.

Now you know my tale
I can't be bothered anymore
To come to school or read or write
I've told you all before.

Chorus:
I'm no good at English
I'm no good at art
And when it comes to numeracy
You couldn't call me smart.

Naomi Taylor (10)
St Peter's Primary School, South Croydon

Daydreams

Mrs Palmer thinks I'm painting
But no
I'm eating ice cream
I'm playing with a mud pie
With three tiny onions in the middle.

Mrs Palmer thinks I'm singing
But no
I'm dancing in a hall
With a load of butterflies
Singing oh so loud.

Mrs Palmer thinks I'm talking
But no
I'm chasing my dog in the sky
With the twinkling stars going by.

Bethany Baden (7)
St Peter's Primary School, South Croydon

My New School

I'm going to a new school,
I'm walking down the hall,
I don't have a friend
And the day's about to end.

I was walking home,
When I walked into a gnome,
And then I lost my shoe,
I didn't know what to do.

When I finally got to my house,
I trod on a woodlouse,
I knocked at the door,
Walked in and fell to the floor.

Belen Tahir (10)
St Peter's Primary School, South Croydon

Nothing But Trouble . . . Mostly!

Dear Headmaster,
Harriet Brown's more than a pain,
One day she will drive me insane!
During maths she fiddles and dreams
And in the playground she shouts and screams.

She bends the rulers until they snap,
She scribbles all over a UK map,
In class she flicks little bits of chalk
And she seems to talk and talk and *talk.*

She tied Judy's plaits to the back of her chair
And when she's told off, she doesn't care,
She wrecked the equipment in the hall
And tore the artwork off the wall.

She teased Sarah about her feet
And put some glue on Mary's seat,
She put George's project in the bin,
I'm fighting a battle I'll never win!

She put Harry's PE kit in the sink
And painted all the class rubbers pink,
Sorry Headmaster, I don't know what to do,
That is why I wrote to you.

I want to know what you've got to say,
Reply soon, perhaps today.
Yours sincerely,
        Mrs White (6W)
PS - The thing is, she's exceptionally bright!

Sophie Ip (11)
St Peter's Primary School, South Croydon

Dear Mrs Taylor

Dear Mrs Taylor,
I'm running away with a sailor
I'm not gonna be at school
So *ssshhh* and don't be cruel
I cut my hand
I'm sure you'll understand
I'm gonna watch Palace
Sitting in an oak tree
2 . . . 4 . . . 6 . . . 8
Who do we appreciate?
Not the king
Not the queen
But Crystal Palace football team
I'll be back Monday
If it's not on Sunday
I'm blinging
You're minging
So don't mess with me
But right now I'm running free
From
Mrs C D Rom
PS I hate you so don't expect me back after all.

Abigail Bates (11)
St Peter's Primary School, South Croydon

Daydreams

Mrs Palmer thinks I'm working,
But I'm playing my PS2.
Mrs Palmer thinks I'm painting,
But I'm playing sword fights with a pirate.
Mrs Palmer thinks I'm writing,
But I'm playing football.
Mrs Palmer thinks I'm reading,
But I'm in a PlayStation game.

Joseph Kabbara (8)
St Peter's Primary School, South Croydon

Day Dream

Mrs Palmer thinks I'm reading
But I'm flying with Peter Pan to Never Land
With my two brothers.
Mrs Palmer thinks I'm listening
But I'm dancing in the moonlight with Iona.
Mrs Palmer thinks I'm working
But I'm shooting out Happy New Year.
Mrs Palmer thinks I'm painting
But I'm camping with Maddy and making scary noises.
Mrs Palmer thinks I'm drawing
But I'm leaving the world.
Mrs Palmer thinks I'm walking
But I'm sunbathing in the sun in Majorca.

Emma Tarrant (7)
St Peter's Primary School, South Croydon

Daydreams

Mrs Palmer thinks I'm reading, but no,
I'm inside a dragon's belly eating cat food,
The dragon's taken me to Venus.

Mrs Palmer thinks I'm listening, but no,
I'm playing football against Neptune,
Earth won one trillion-nil.
Now I am playing against New York in basketball
But the Looney Tunes won instead of New York.

Mrs Palmer thinks I'm painting, but no,
I'm in a rainforest swinging on bananas
And playing with baboons,
And that's that.

Jason Ying (8)
St Peter's Primary School, South Croydon

Daydreams

Mrs Palmer thinks I am reading,
But no, I am eating a toenail, foxtail sandwich,
Or casting funny spells on Jason.
I am on telly playing the part of Woody Woodpecker,
Or fighting in the army.
Mrs Palmer thinks I am listening,
But no, I am riding on a grasshopper,
Or being a pop star.
I am taking over as the teacher,
I am being J K Rowling,
Or I am swimming with Nemo.
Mrs Palmer thinks I am writing,
But no, I am the letter A,
Or I am going to China.
I am skating on the moon,
Or I am playing on a spider's web.
I have won £500,000!
Mrs Palmer thinks I am painting,
But no, I am playing tennis with a mouse,
Or riding on an eagle.
I am the paintbrush,
Or I am eating the paint.
I am in a circus.
Next time you daydream in school,
Maybe you will dream about all those things that I did.

Lucy Wordsworth (8)
St Peter's Primary School, South Croydon

Daydreams

Mrs Palmer thinks I'm playing,
But no, I'm in a haunted house,
I'm riding a ghost,
I'm making a spell,
I'm playing in the dark black room,
I'm riding high on a witch's broomstick.

Mrs Palmer thinks I'm reading,
But no, I'm in the lazy farm,
I'm riding the red bull,
I'm milking the alien cow,
I'm dancing with the silly sheepdog.

Mrs Palmer thinks I'm eating,
But no, I'm having a times table sandwich,
I'm having mashed potato cloud,
I'm having splendid slime,
I'm eating dragon's fire.

Mrs Palmer thinks I'm working,
But no, I'm having a snow fight on the moon,
I'm watching the moon turn into chocolate,
I'm playing Romans on the moon,
I'm boxing on the moon,
I'm eating the planets,
Are you?

Serena Williams (7)
St Peter's Primary School, South Croydon

Daydreams

Mrs Palmer thinks I'm feeding the fish,
But no, I'm swimming with the fish and tasting all their food,
I'm dreaming of eating a candyfloss cloud whilst floating above
                                                    the trees,
I'm driving a bright red racing car, soon I win the race,
I'm trapped in a bubble and drift high into space.
Mrs Palmer thinks I'm reading,
But no, I'm still flying in the sky and looking at the world passing by,
I got to space and went skiing on the planets and at the moon
                                        because it was cheese,
And I sunbathed on the sun and got brown all over.
Mrs Palmer thinks I'm listening,
But no, I'm surfing on chocolate sauce and eating the chocolate
                                            on the way,
I'm lying in cold water to cool off my hot, burnt back,
I can see Nemo swimming around in my bath,
He came to the surface and squirted water on my face,
I said to Nemo, 'Thank you, that cooled me down a lot.'
Nemo said, You're most welcome.'
Mrs Palmer said, 'Write what you like in your writing journals.'
We said, 'OK miss.'
Can you guess what I wrote about?
Yes, I wrote about what I daydreamed in class.
I always daydream.

Isabelle Wallin-Trapp (8)
St Peter's Primary School, South Croydon

Daydreams

Mrs Palmer thinks I'm reading
But no
I'm skydiving down the corridor
Or boxing a water book.

Mrs Palmer thinks I'm working
But no
I'm eating a lightbulb
Or floating in a bubble.

Mrs Palmer thinks I'm painting
But no
I'm drinking the piano keys.

Mrs Palmer thinks I'm listening
But no
I'm eating a chocolate volcano with orange lava
Or wearing glasses on my head.

Mrs Palmer thinks I'm doing art
But no
I'm in a temple in China with the Chinese animals.

Mrs Palmer thinks I'm doing homework
But no
I'm sleeping on the tap.

Shannon Taylor (8)
St Peter's Primary School, South Croydon

Day Dreams

Mrs Palmer thinks I'm reading, but no,
I'm exploring the rainforest,
I'm putting on a super costume to help me fly and soar.

Mrs Palmer thinks I'm listening, but no,
I'm riding on a dragon's back,
I'm swinging through the trees with monkeys.

Mrs Palmer thinks I'm working, but no,
I'm snowboarding in space,
I'm in another dimension fighting a jaguar.

My imagination flows.

Taban Stroude (8)
St Peter's Primary School, South Croydon

Daydreams

Mrs Palmer thinks that I'm reading
But I'm not, I'm eating a book,
I'm flying like a bird,
I'm on Mars with an invisible man,
I'm having a dragon for my tea.

Mrs Palmer thinks I'm working
But I'm not, I'm having spiders
And ants and rats
And potatoes with toes and toenails.
I'm under the floorboards,
I'm in the window,
I'm inside the radiator,
I'm having wiggly worms for my drink.

Amber Smith (7)
St Peter's Primary School, South Croydon

Daydreams

Mrs Palmer thinks I'm reading,
But I'm not,
I've been eaten by an elephant,
I'm stuck in a keyhole,
I might be part of a PlayStation game
Called Tyrannosaurus Rex.
Mrs Palmer thinks I'm listening,
But I'm on a pencil sharpener,
Skiing on the moon,
Or pulling my dad's hair out,
Or I might be playing sun hockey on the sun.
Mrs Palmer thinks I'm working,
But I'm not,
I'm in someone's brain,
Pulling their times table numbers out,
Or I'm digging a hole under the ground
And I slept there or I rode an eagle.
Mrs Palmer thinks I'm painting,
But I'm not,
I'm thinking about swimming with sharks,
Or surfboarding on a ruler,
I might be living on a pole.

Ryan Sibbald (7)
St Peter's Primary School, South Croydon

Daydreams

Mrs Palmer thinks I'm concentrating on the Romans,
But I'm knocking Caesar head first into a ditch,
Living inside Vesuvius,
Dropping a CD Rom into my tummy so I can play stuff in there,
(press my belly button to start and stop),
Chucking the sun over the hill.
Mrs Palmer thinks I'm . . . laughing . . . with *no* fear.

Jordan Glass (7)
St Peter's Primary School, South Croydon

Daydreams

Mrs Palmer thinks I'm working, but I'm not,
I'm thinking of being a shark.
Mrs Palmer thinks I'm reading, but I'm not,
I'm thinking of having a pet dinosaur.
Mrs Palmer thinks I'm painting, but I'm not,
I'm thinking that the sea is Coke.
Mrs Palmer thinks I'm singing, but I'm not,
I'm thinking of flying into space.
Mrs Palmer thinks I'm listening, but I'm not,
I'm thinking of pizza made out of Weetos.
Mrs Palmer thinks I'm sitting up nicely, but I'm not,
I'm thinking of chocolate cake made out of wet, brown paper,
With chocolate sauce on top.
Do you do this?

George Harman (7)
St Peter's Primary School, South Croydon

Day Dreams

Mrs Palmer thinks I'm listening,
No, I'm not,
I'm fighting a basilisk,
I'm skating off a cliff,
I'm in World War I and II,
I'm 006 in the 2004 007 game
'Everything Or Nothing' on my PlayStation,
I'm surfing in space,
I'm eating a gun cake with lava inside,
I'm 001 in 'The Spy Who Loved Me'
With a licence to kill.

Samuel Lovell (7)
St Peter's Primary School, South Croydon

Daydreams

Mrs Palmer thinks I'm listening
But no
I'm eating toenails with cake stuck inside
Or drinking mud and worms in a bottle full of ice.

Mrs Palmer thinks I'm working
But no
I'm sleeping on slimy slugs
Or relaxing in beetle juice.

Mrs Palmer thinks I'm sunbathing on the table
But no
I'm playing chicken with Mars and Venus
Or swimming in dragon soup.

Mrs Palmer thinks I'm on holiday
But no
I'm making mud pies
Or sleeping in a cement mixer.

Gemma Dewhurst (7)
St Peter's Primary School, South Croydon

Daydreams

Mrs Palmer thinks I'm reading, but no,
I'm jumping on a huge peach,
I'm playing ice hockey on Pluto,
I'm stuck in a tree.
Mrs Palmer thinks I'm listening, but no,
I'm sunbathing in the sun,
I'm playing on the computer,
I'm in a book.
Mrs Palmer thinks I'm painting, but no,
I'm kicking a ball
While I'm eating a meat sandwich.

Iona Leigh (7)
St Peter's Primary School, South Croydon

Daydreams

Mrs Palmer thinks I'm listening,
But I'm drawing a girl called Clover
And I become her.
I float up to space and turn into a camel.
Mrs Palmer thinks I'm working,
But I've been sucked into the soil bag,
I've been pulled in from a book,
Now I am part of the book.
Mrs Palmer thinks I'm reading,
But I'm eating caterpillar sandwiches.
Mrs Palmer thinks I'm painting,
But I'm in the picture.

Maryam Haque (7)
St Peter's Primary School, South Croydon

My Recipe For A Brilliant Book

Ingredients
7 compelling pages
1 cup of mild action
18 spoons of wonderful toons
A cup of hilarious humour
180 grams of imaginative nouns
Lots of fantastic words
A cooking pan
The name of your book

Method
First get a cooking pan, and throw in 7 compelling
pages, and leave for 5 minutes.
Next add lots of fantastic words and stir.
While stirring, add 180 grams of
wonderful pictures.
Now add a cup of mild action and 180 grams
of imaginative nouns.
Now say the name of your book and boil for 2 hours.

Jamie Woods (9)
Stanley Park Junior School

Claudina's Recipe For A Wonderful Book

Ingredients
100g of adventure juice,
Two evil characters on the loose
2 sums of fiction
A bag full of disruption
2½ packages of History
And gallons and gallons of mystery
A plain book
With old Captain Hook.

Method:
Get the plain book
And tip in Captain Hook.
Mix in the 2½ packages of History,
Don't use all the mystery.
Pour in some adventure juice,
And tip in the evil characters on the loose.
Add the sums of fiction
Don't forget the disruption.

Claudina Vaz (9)
Stanley Park Junior School

Imagine Animals

Imagine a giraffe as long-necked
as a massive diplodocus eating plants.

Imagine a cheetah as quick as an email
that arrives rapidly.

Imagine a zebra as stripy as a piano,
with black and white stripes that really dazzle you.

Imagine an ostrich twittering round
like a mad crazy bird.

Imagine the cows grazing in the fields
for what seems forever in a second!

Bijal Shukla (9)
Stanley Park Junior School

Lois' Recipe For A Fabulous Book

Ingredients
1 exciting paragraph
2 mysterious plots
3 descriptive nouns
4 suspenseful characters
5 dazzling endings
6 sparkling adjectives.

Method:
Start with an exciting paragraph, don't forget to cut it in half.
Put it in a bowl, check it doesn't have a hole.
Get 2 mysterious plots, cook it, don't make it too hot.
Take 3 descriptive nouns, but remember don't mix them in
with towns.
4 suspenseful characters, you can get them in Sainsbury's
For just 10 pence.
5 dazzling endings, don't worry there's no more spending.
6 twinkling adjectives, hold them up or they'll keep sinking.
Give it a mix, then leave it to sit
Your book is done, so read it and have fun.

Lois Baker (9)
Stanley Park Junior School

Paris

Oh! go on the Eiffel Tower
Or have a crêpe
Have a romantic dinner,
Or have a cheesecake,
Have some adventures at Disneyland.
You'll get worn out so go home to bed.
The next day do the same thing,
But have some frogs legs and wine and snails,
Then have a look at the Arc de Triumph and the Seine.

Eleanor Pullen (8)
Stanley Park Junior School

A Recipe For A Good Book

Michael was a fine young lad
As he went through the library with his fine young dad.
He opened a book, looked inside,
'It looks good, brilliant' he cried.
Read a page looking up and down
His mouth curled into a frown.

Ingredients:
1 pot of mystery
2 dishes of History.
Some words weighing about a tonne
Also you need plenty of fun.

Method:
Pour in the one pot of mystery
And 2 dishes of History.
Leave to simmer until goes blue
Yamadidamadido
Put in the words only a tonne
Then sprinkle in plenty of fun.

'What could the recipe be for?'
Said Michael in lots of awe,
'I wish I could know, but I can't, oh blow!'
'I really, really, really doubt I'll ever find out
What this book's about.'
He put it back with a thwack
And never ever came back.

Matthew Blow (10)
Stanley Park Junior School

Imagine

Imagine a giraffe as tall as a tree
licking his nose and eating some leaves.

Imagine a cheetah as fast as a train
so beware he may out run you in a car.

Imagine a zebra all stripy and proud
he gallops like a horse and all black and white.

Imagine an ostrich tall and happy
running like a car gracefully and proud.

Imagine the cows skinny or fat give lovely milk
grazing on the field eating the lush green grass.

Imagine the antelope galloping across cornfields
running from the deadly predator.

Daniel Browne (9)
Stanley Park Junior School

Imagine

Imagine a giraffe as tall as can be
chasing through the leaves as easy as can be.

Imagine a cheetah rough and tough
speeding without even a puff.

Imagine a zebra stripy and white
galloping through without a fright.

Imagine an ostrich as fast as can be
it would totally whizz past me.

Imagine the cows lazy and fat
suddenly they are laying flat on a mat.

Imagine the antelope horny and fast
the cheetah catches it, so it's last.

George O'Neill (9)
Stanley Park Junior School

Kapiti Plain

Imagine a giraffe as tall as can be
with a neck that's long and four legs that are strong.

Imagine a cheetah that's vicious and fast
who make people jump when he runs past.

Imagine a zebra who can gallop and graze
like a horse with stripes that are black and white.

Imagine an ostrich who has a long neck
and has a big beak ready to peck.

Imagine the cows lazy and plump with a swinging tail
but when they moo they make people jump.

Imagine the antelope that's leaping with joy
when he sees danger his joy is destroyed.

Mark Richards (9)
Stanley Park Junior School

Kapiti Plain

On the plain
the cow is being lazy.
On the plain
the cheetah is joyful.
On the plain
the giraffe is quiet.
On the plain
the zebra eats green grass.
On the plain
the antelope is deer-like.
On the plain
the ostrich is as fast as the wind.
On the plain
the snake is hissing.

Emine Sayan (8)
Stanley Park Junior School

Imagine

Imagine a giraffe as tall as can be,
yellow and brown eating the leaves off the tree.

Imagine a cheetah as fast as can be,
all spotty and orange, running with glee.

Imagine a zebra stripy all over
like an old fashioned TV with no colour.

Imagine an ostrich as speedy as can be,
with very long legs to run with and a long neck.

Imagine the cows mooing away all spotty and white
praying for rain.

Imagine the antelope being chased by the cheetah,
caught, frightened and weak.

Harry Short (8)
Stanley Park Junior School

My Ideal Book

Take a family and a mouse

Give them furniture and a house

Make them happy
Make them work
Make them go on a quest.

Stir in lots of descriptive words . . .
Make your book the best

Then put in a villain, that gets defeated
By a hero.

Add more people, friend or foe!

But really make sure you like your book

And all you need to do now is cook, cook, cook!

Megan Harrison (10)
Stanley Park Junior School

Fantastic Book

Take a girl and her father who loves books
And mix them up with a mystery.
Add the father's history
And you've got a
Great
Book.

Include a villain who wants to kill them
And wouldn't do anything 'til he does.
And you've got a
Fabulous
Book.

Lock them up in prison,
Where did the villain come from?
He was risen from a book
Called Ink Heart.
Look at these facts
This is what I want in a
Fantastic
Book.

Jodie Atwell (9)
Stanley Park Junior School

The One Ring

A glittering house upon a hill
Down in a canyon everything still.
In the house of Elrond everything quiet
Away in Mordor there is a riot.
Between mankind and black riders,
Down they swoop like huge looming gliders.

Over the one ring that is held by a Hobbit,
That wants to throw it into the fires of Mt Doom.
Mt Doom is incredibly tall
Frodo has the one ring
The one ring to rule them all.

Jacob Ketcher (10)
Stanley Park Junior School

My Ideal Book

(Based on 'The Suitcase Kid' by Jacqueline Wilson)

Take a family, stir them up.

Make them argue, split them up.

Get a girl and a rabbit.

Make her nice with no bad habits.

Add some noise, with a shout.

Mix them round, don't let them out.

Include some houses 1, 2, 3.

Don't forget the family.

Add some cousins for some fun.

Make them go, for a run.

Then all you do is cook, cook, cook.

This is what I think makes a good book.

Jasmine Rajagopalan (10)
Stanley Park Junior School

A Good Book

A recipe for a good book
Take a hypnotism teacher, tell her to wear a
cape and underpants
Put him in a city
Let him fight a villain
Have a hideout for the villain
Let the kids follow the years
The teacher will fight for truth
and justice
Put them altogether, you get a good book
called Captain Underpants
They are my favourite.

Andrew Cross (10)
Stanley Park Junior School

That's What I Call Cold Winter Days

Reindeers and huskies pulling big sleighs
with bells and holly on the sleighs
jingle bells and prickly holly
that's what I call cold winter days.

Back in the house with a warm burning fire,
go up to bed to an early start,
tomorrow will bring some great winning prizes,
just go up to bed and wake in the morning.

Go outside and build a big snowman
Then throw snowballs at people passing by
now off I go out with my friends
and go ice-skating on the frozen water.

At lunchtime I can't wait to go out
on the sleighs to see black and white huskies
and bronze brown reindeers to ride on
to see the great horns and feed them for the rest of the day.

That's what I call cold winter days,
go home to bed and dream of the things I've done,
and that's another day gone
because that's what I call cold winter days,
because that's what I call cold winter days.
I'm going home tomorrow to leave the cold winter days.

Rebecca Hall (9)
Stanley Park Junior School

To The Land Of Peace

On the plane he went,
To the land of peace,
Happy as can be,
To the land of peace.
Happy as can be,
To the land of peace,
New York, New York, New York,
To the land of peace.

Katherine Woollett (8)
Stanley Park Junior School

My Recipe For A Good Book

Mix 34 cups of imagination,
With 40g of great description,
Stir and mix until green,
Remember to keep your fingers clean!

Stir 20g of humour around,
To make you laugh and make some sound,
Also 100ml of suspense,
To keep you feeling very tense!

Add 120g of wonderful pages,
To keep you hooked on this for ages,
Put interesting powder into the pot,
And very slowly stir the lot.

Now you've got everything for a perfect read,
You have all the ingredients you need,
It will be so much fun
And now it's totally finished and done!

Shivani Rathod (9)
Stanley Park Junior School

A Recipe For A Good Book

Ten cups of action
One cup of reaction
Five joke books
Sprinkled on notebooks
Then put in five eyes
That are still alive
Then pour a cup of pages
And stay and watch for ages
Slowly walk with your recipe
But if you're not careful
There may be a catastrophe.

Joslyn Whiteman (9)
Stanley Park Junior School

My Ingredients For A Good Book

The ingredients you need . . .
50g of villains full of greed
A sprinkle of dastardly plots
Add a handful of dragons covered in spots
Don't forget the 65mm of heroes, fantastic magic
Finally the cup of endings, don't make them tragic.
Leave for one hour
Until it goes sour
Then put them in a cave
To make the heroes brave
Lastly in the stove
To turn the dragons colour mauve
Now your book should be great
If it's not out of date.

Thomas Grimes (10)
Stanley Park Junior School

My Own Book

M ystery, action that's my book
Y ummy, yummy gingerbread men that's also my book

O range people that's funny but it's my book
W ords and verbs that's so my book
N aughty children that's my book

B ulky men that is my book
O ats and sweets that's really my book
O ctopus is cool but it's *sooo* my book
K ind children that's not my book.

James Painter (9)
Stanley Park Junior School

My Jolly Old Recipe For A Jolly Book

Two or three sheets of sugar paper
One bowl of ink, must be sweet.
Start mixing the ink and put cornflour in.
Leave it to rest
So the ink will go on the sweet paper.
After a few minutes get your bowl of full stops
When you've done that get the whole box of nouns,
Imagination, description,
Adjectives, punctuation, adverbs,
Pictures and finally action.
Put in the oven, leave for two hours
Take it out and it should look like a big book.
Don't eat yet because you have to put it in the fridge overnight,
And you'll have a smiley face and a jolly old good cake.

Sabrina Porter (10)
Stanley Park Junior School

Australia

A koala comes waving bye
U nder the table comes a kangaroo
S unny and bright is the mood
T en wombats come flying with food
R unning in the garden are three koalas
A nd peacefully and gracefully they pass the kangaroo
L ounging beside the swimming pool
I 'm soaking up the sun
A nd enjoying my Australia by having lots of fun.

Onzo Izuchukwu (9)
Stanley Park Junior School

Emma's Recipe For A Magnificent Book

Start off with 26 tablespoons of excitement and plots,
It encourages me to read, lots and lots.

Pour in the imagination sprinkles
Stay up late reading until the stars twinkle.

Add the 20g of verbs and nouns
Describe the cities and towns.

Remember your punctuation and speech marks
Add detail for streets and parks.

Are your characters thin or fat?
What do they wear? A scarf and a hat?

Leave it for six hours to bake and stew
You have now got a book that's brand new.

Emma Holder (10)
Stanley Park Junior School

A Book

A book can be as boring as an old boot
or as fun as a toot from Mrs Armatinge's bike

A book can have a picture with great detail
or a sketch by Quentin Blake.

A book thick by Shakespeare
or a ladybird book about a deer.

A book can be sad
or a mad fighting story.

Francesca Chapman (9)
Stanley Park Junior School

A Wonderful Book

Here are some ingredients to make your book great.

3g of evil, 3g of hate
A sprinkle of good and monster hairy
5 spoons of all things very scary
Dozens of good paragraphs
10g of humour to make you laugh
8oz of adjectives make your story exciting
A tablespoon of battles and of fighting

Now for the method to do the making

Get ready for some cooking and baking
First add evil and hate, 3 grams of each
A mysterious wizard with poisonous peach
Next spread this mixture over your compelling pages
Stir in some action, your mixture will go pink
Sprinkle some mystery to make you think
Next put in 14g of plot
Cook till your story goes hot
Now add some adventure good or scary
Stir in weird creatures and monsters hairy
Scrape in dozens of good paragraphs
Don't forget 10g of humour to make you laugh
Important are adjectives to make your story exciting
Next add a tablespoon of battles and of fighting
Now your mixture will be the colour of a seed
At last your story's ready to read!

Poppy Large (10)
Stanley Park Junior School

A Super Fab Recipe For A Fab Book!

Ingredients
2 cups of fab and wonderful nouns
3 tablespoons of creative sounds
13 characters maybe detectives
A cup of personality maybe protective
6 teacups of creative adjectives
4 mixing bowls of words and fun
7 small bowls of imagination make
your readers minds run
2 big cups of paragraphs
Make your book real laughs!
11 huge cups of pages
6 pinches of jokes and phrases.

Method
First put 5 cups of pages into the mixing bowl.
Then add 6 pinches of phrases
Leave for ten minutes, it seems like ages.
Next add 13 characters, maybe detectives
Stir on personality maybe protective
Then add 6 teacups of creative adjectives
Next add 4 big bowls of words and fun
7 small bowls of imagination
Make your readers minds run
Stir in 2 cups of fab and wonderful nouns
Sprinkle in 12 tablespoons of creative sounds.

Jade Le Gendre (9)
Stanley Park Junior School

What You Need For A Good Book

Pinch of pages
A cup of drama
A teaspoon of interesting adjectives
A cup of pictures in mind
A pinch of mystery to find
But no literacy
I suppose a teaspoon of history
A cup of neat writing
Then a pinch of spooky lightning
A cup of fun
But after the lightning a teaspoon of sun
A cup of humour
Pour in the lot till it gets hot
When bubble starts bubbling
Start stirring then get learning
Then a pinch of happy ending.

Suzanna Wells (9)
Stanley Park Junior School

Winter

We put on our coats
Our gloves, scarves and also hats
We look at the snow.

We walk on the field
To have a big snowball fight
I throw the snowballs.

It's time to go in
We take off our coats and hats
Also scarves and gloves.

Thomas McDonald (11)
Stanley Park Junior School

Snow

Watch all the snow falling,
Everywhere snow is settling,
On the ground.
Children all go outside to play,
In the snow.

Hear the crunching sound,
Of the snow as children,
Run, hop, jump, skip and walk.

Children having snowball fights,
All the cold snowballs hitting you
As you run away from them.

Then it's time to go inside
And have a lovely hot drink
To warm you up.
As the snow starts to melt away.

Victoria Constantinou (10)
Stanley Park Junior School

Duck, Roll, Throw

Duck, duck, duck,
Duck to avoid a snowball,
Roll, roll, roll,
Roll a snowball round and solid.
Throw, throw, throw,
Throw with all your might.
Hit, hit, hit,
Give yourself a pat on the back
That's the way,
That's the way,
That's the way to enjoy the snow.

Harry Frost (10)
Stanley Park Junior School

Snow Poem

Snow is white,
Snow is beautiful,
The only thing it's not,
Is colourful.
Snow is cold,
Makes fingers like ice.
Freshly fallen snow,
Looks really nice.
Walk in it, play in it, roll it in a ball,
Come on snow, we want more to fall.

Stephen Foss (10)
Stanley Park Junior School

Snowfall

Snow is falling from the sky
Watching them from your little eye
See them fall gently on the ground

> The snow is crunchy
> All sparkling white
> Very few of the flakes are really
> *Bright!*

The snow is soft
It's fun to catch them on your tongue
People love playing in the snow
Taking big steps to and fro.

> The children shout

'We all love the snow!'

Louis Collingwood (11)
Stanley Park Junior School

I Like Snow I Like It Not

Snow blocks roads
Snow freezes fish
Snow creates avalanches

Snow is fab.

I used to think snow was rotten
I thought it should be forever forgotten
Until that is I threw a snowball
At my sister
Unfortunately, I missed her.

Now, I think snow is great -
It's the best thing I've ever had.
Carrying on our snowball fight

She threw a snowball back at me -
I dodged.
I threw another back at her
I got her this time that's for sure.
That's why snow is best of all!

Lydia Murtezaoglu (10)
Stanley Park Junior School

Snow Poem

The snow falls on the ground
The children played around
Snow's not bad
So just go mad
In the wonderful, crunchy snow!

Hallam Rickett (10)
Stanley Park Junior School

A Winter's Tale

Snowflakes tumbling, gritter trucks rumbling.
Snowballs flying, small girls crying.
Drivers complaining, happiness waning.
People sliding, warm weather hiding.
Temperatures dropping, sunshine stopping.
Blizzards falling, babies bawling.
This is my hope for each and every year
For a winter without snow is my greatest fear.

Kathryn Mossor (11)
Stanley Park Junior School

Snow

Snow is made out of water that
Looks like icing on a cake but softer.
When water gets to snow
It turns into wet ice
Which makes it very hard to play with.
When ice melts
The snow is no longer with us.
Snow is falling,
Children are playing,
Schools are shut, roads are wet.
People having snowball fights.
Snowmen in every garden.
Night is coming
Children are tired as dogs
More fun will be had in the morning when they wake up.
On the cold winter's day
All the snow has gone,
It was such a disappointment.
The children cried and cried
When their masterpieces were destroyed.

Jonathan Davies (10)
Stanley Park Junior School

I Love Books

Books, books, books
I can't get enough.
Books, books, books,
Are never rough.
Books, books, books,
I'll read any one.
Books, books, books,
Even if they're about sums.

Humour books, humour books
Make me *laugh.*
Horror books, horror books,
Scare me *stiff.*
Fact books, fact books
Are very *fascinating.*
Adventure books, adventure books
Are never boring.

Can I tell you something?

I love, I love,
I love,
Books.

Max Collins (10)
Stanley Park Junior School

Australia

There are kangaroos
And people work very hard too.
There are snakes in Australia
Poor people live in huts
The rich people live in big houses
There are weird looking insects
Like snakes, and weird looking spiders.
The poor people drink dirty water
And they have to eat animals because they
don't have any food.

Paige Magorrian (8)
Stanley Park Junior School

It Happens Every Year

It happens every year
St Valentine's Day is here
There's Cupid with his bow and arrow
And Venus with her singing sparrow.

It happens every year
St Valentine's Day is here
When people fall in love
And Venus with her singing dove.

It happens every year
St Valentine's Day is here
Some people think it's absurd
It's not, there's Venus with her singing bird.

It happens every year
St Valentine's Day is here
When people give out gifts
I hope it will last forever that's my wish.

It happens every year
St Valentine's Day is here
The day is here again
There will never be an end
Yes, never go round the bend.

Eloise Bowden (8)
Stanley Park Junior School

Snow In Scotland

S now is always in northern Scotland
C areful on the ice
O ccasionally someone trips but then they are all right
T eachers always say be careful but the children do not care
L ovely snow! Everyone says
A mazing, amazing, amazing
N obody hates the snow
D o not stay indoors, go out and play!

Laura McDonald (9)
Stanley Park Junior School

A Recipe For A Good Book

Persuade the reader
with a thriller
convince them
that it's brill.

Make them see
and dance with glee,
that this is a
wonderful mystery

Include some classics
make it magic
have some fun with
the story.

Now that's the end
of a wonderful book
the puzzle is solved
'Just one more'
'No!'

Hollie Prentice (9)
Stanley Park Junior School

African Plain

The spotted fast cheetah ran around
the dry grass.
Rapidly he moves with intense speed,
never stopping.
Searching around and through the high imposing
grass for food.
Pounce!
Poor antelope is super
away he sprints at high speed.

Wayne Gyamfi (8)
Stanley Park Junior School

Books Are The Best

Scary books, scary books,
Horror books, horror books,
Classic books, classic books
They are the best.

Books about spies
Books about agents
Books about rescuers
They are the best.

Books about heroes
Books about villains
Books about faraway lands
They are great.

But the very best
Aren't any of them
It's an adventure story
They are brilliant.

Ben Harvey (10)
Stanley Park Junior School

Kapiti Plain

Imagine the long necked giraffe munching
leaves slowly.
Imagine the zebra grazing hungrily on
the fresh green grass.
Imagine the cheetah as fast as a car
prowling the plain for a tasty snack.
Imagine the antelope scared and timid
their feet are strong and their horns are long.

Olivia Guild (9)
Stanley Park Junior School

A Great Book

My book has to have
Mystery and humour
But my favourite has to be
Horror
With a little bit of drama
That's what's right for me

If I had to choose
Which would be the best
It would have to be
Quests and a bit of spies,
And don't forget magic
And also sudden happenings.
Keep the reader in suspense,
That's what's right for me.

If you have a little adventure
Mix it with some pictures
Grab a boy, put him in,
Give him a friend,
Give him food and some shelter,
Now that's my kind of book.

Ben Hale-Jones (9)
Stanley Park Junior School

Spain

S pain is lovely
P aella is great
A nd I love the view
 I n the hotel it was yummy food
N ever rained, the sun was out.

Lisa Crow (9)
Stanley Park Junior School

My Book Poem

A very perfect book
has to have action
adventures and super heroes
in it to get people to read it.

Sometimes everyone knows
that it will have some villains
and monsters in the story
with the other bits.
Adventure story and fairy tales
they are not just good for girls
and boys, they are great.

Fairy tales books are for girls.
Adventure books are for boys
But we might like reading older books
but still we just like reading
All books!

Samuel Gray (9)
Stanley Park Junior School

Underpants

Underpants
Everywhere
I can't find my underwear
Anywhere.
Underpants are a world
Underpants make you fly
My ones are special they can cry
So the next time you put your pants on think
Fly, fly, fly.
May the pants be with you!

Louis Ray (10)
Stanley Park Junior School

Imagine

Imagine a giraffe as tall as a tree
eating green leaves as fast as can be.

Imagine a cheetah as fast as a car
all of a sudden he's eating a
chocolate bar.

Imagine a zebra eating grass and all
of a sudden he's drinking from a glass.

Imagine an ostrich as vicious as a biting hand,
all of a sudden he's playing in the sand.

Imagine the cows as lazy as can be
all of a sudden he's being chased by a bee.

Imagine the antelope with horns as sharp as knives
all of a sudden he's lost all his lives.

Samantha Hall (9)
Stanley Park Junior School

On The Plain

On the plain
the cheetahs run as fast as the speed of light.

On the plain
the zebra trots and grazes on the grass.

On the plain
the cows lay down as lazy as can be.

On the plain
the ostrich strides across the field.

On the plain
the antelope is brown with sharp horns.

On the plain
the giraffe is tall with a long neck.

Taylor Felton (9)
Stanley Park Junior School

Imagine

Imagine a giraffe as slow as a tortoise
if they weren't very tall they'd have nothing to eat.

Imagine a cheetah all spotted and sleek
his tummy is rumbling, he's having something to eat.

Imagine a zebra all full with stripes
its victims are hungry so they've got to be quick.

Imagine an ostrich with black and white feathers
soft as a cushion but as vicious as a lion.

Imagine the cows saying moo moo moo
the cows are proud of their language and we're
proud of them too.

Imagine the antelope with its big sharp horns
if you mess with him, you'll wish you were never born.

Tim Brann (8)
Stanley Park Junior School

Imagine

Imagine a giraffe as tall
as the Eiffel Tower.

Imagine a cheetah as fast
as a rocket, if you're lucky you might see it.

Imagine a zebra,
it eats grass and has stripes.

Imagine an ostrich,
it has a long neck to eat from trees.

Imagine the cows, they eat grass
and they have black and white spots.

Imagine the antelope, it eats from the grass
and if a cheetah sees it, it will chase it.

James De Brunner (8)
Stanley Park Junior School

On The Plain

On the plain
the giraffe travels slowly across the hot, dry land.

On the plain
the long necked ostrich speeds proudly on the
fresh green grass.

On the plain
the swift, spotty cheetah runs quicker than any new, fast car.

On the plain
the zebra grazes gracefully on the fresh bright grass.

On the plain
the worried antelope runs as fast as he can away from
the fast, hungry predator.

On the plain
the proud, observant eagle soars lightly over the hot,
hot land.

On the plain
the hidden lion is searching for fresh, tasty food.

Catherine Cheng (9)
Stanley Park Junior School

Jammin' In Jamaica!

J ammin' to reggae music
A qua sports on every beach
M angoes sweet and juicy
A cool long cocktail made especially for me.
I dyllic scenery
C oconuts galore
A ll adds up to the best holiday!

Sean Reilly (9)
Stanley Park Junior School

Imagine

Imagine a giraffe as tall as a shed
Munching leaves inside its mouth.

Imagine a cheetah as fast as a plane,
Racing a leopard across the lake.

Imagine a zebra galloping like horses
Trotting free along the tall grass.

Imagine an ostrich with very long legs
Running as fast as the wind, flapping feathers everywhere.

Imagine the cows black and white
Giving milk to people who need it.

Imagine the antelope with long horns
Bashing a tree with its wired horns.

Nithin Thoppuram (8)
Stanley Park Junior School

Kapiti Plain

On the plain
the cow was mooing for water.

On the plain
the snake was creepy.

On the plain
the cheetah was so vicious and if he sees any
animals he jumps on them.

On the plain
the giraffe has got a long neck to reach the leaves.

On the plain
the ostrich is black, vicious and big.

On the plain
the zebra is stripy.

Lee Taylor (9)
Stanley Park Junior School

Books Are The Best

Books are fantastic
Books are great fun
Read lots of books
And you'll be impressed!

Read humorous books
Read mystery books
Read books with villains in
And read books with heroes in!

I love reading
And looking at the pictures
Sometimes they make me laugh
Or sometimes they give me a fright!

I like adventure stories
And magical books
I like books with chapters
And fairy tales too.

Kerri Haines (9)
Stanley Park Junior School

My South Africa

S oaking wet rhinos getting cool
O striches at the drinking pool
U p in the clouds are the birds
T he elephants always travel in herds
H appy hippos in the shade.

A clear blue sky starts to fade
F reedom roams around the land
R hinos giving the lions a hand
I t's always really warm and sunny
C ooking sometimes tastes quite funny
A nd you should really go there.

George Driscoll (9)
Stanley Park Junior School

Author Advice

A book that is my type
Would have to be Northern Lights
With other world
And girls with curls
Books are always different.

Classics are also to my taste
With awful places with rubbish and waste
Write a book with a convincing quest
To make the reader think you're the best.

Include some magic now and then,
Mermaids and sharks with dark, dark dens.
Make your reader wonder what's on the next page,
Not think *this book goes on for an age!*

And last make an appropriate ending
With a spooky path that is twisting and bending.
Write a book like the Subtle Knife
Just please take my advice.

Georgina Howes (10)
Stanley Park Junior School

Fishing

Fishing, oh fishing
How good can this get?
Put a wiggling, waggling maggot
On my hook.
Catching a carp
How good can this get?
Weighing and releasing it
Letting it go.

Charlie Bone (10)
Stanley Park Junior School

Books

Books are the best
Better than the rest
Mystery books or
History books
They are better than all the rest.

Books, so good you can't put them down.
Books so funny they make you fall down.
They are better than all the rest.

All these books you can't put them down
They are so good, you read and read,
Until you come to the end
And you won't read it over again.
Just like the Harry Potter books
They are better than all the rest.

Books with dripping horror
Books with mysteries
Books with drama
Books with puzzles
All these books make a good book.
They are better than all the rest.

Ashley Gopee (10)
Stanley Park Junior School

Animals

Animals scuttering past the plants,
Birds are swooping, diving fast,
Trees are swaying through the night,
The glorious sun glows at half-past nine,
You see the cheetahs sprinting fast,
While the rabbits are leapfrogging past.

Francesca Newman (11)
Stanley Park Junior School

The Shark

The shark circles you round and round
He can't live on the hot dry ground
When he comes, he scares all the fish away
Lots of worried faces for another day.
He has been called, so you'd better be warned
When he is there you can't see him,
All you can see is his big pointy fin.
You see it going round and round
Then *snap* the next thing you see
Is the inside of his stomach.

Drew Beckley (11)
Stanley Park Junior School

My Little Brother

(Dedicated to my little brother Zack)

My little brother is a pain,
I want to give him a great big cane.
His punch is very hard,
He can kick me over a yard.

His bite leaves a mark,
He ruins my shoes from Clarks.
His pinch really stings,
He won't let me touch his things.

He always has yummy sweets,
Also he has smelly feet.
He wants to do karate,
And be a right smarty.

Although he's a pain,
He has no shame.
Annoying as he can be,
All I can say is . . .
I love him!

Kathryn Streatfield (10)
Stanley Park Junior School

After Ever Happily

After ever happily
The princess killed the prince
They had many arguments
Then she turned him into mince.

After ever happily
Red Riding Hood was brunch
The wolf came back to life
Tomorrow Grandma's for lunch.

After ever happily
Cinderella smashed her shoes
They gave her awful blisters
Now that she was on the booze.

After ever happily
Pan lost his gift of flight
Hook learnt how to fly
And he took off like a kite.

Brittany Edmondson-Jones (11)
Stanley Park Junior School

Opposite

There's a girl in our class called Opposite,
She always does everything the contrary way.
When we come into school in mufti,
She comes in school uniform.
When we put sticky gel on our hair,
She just leaves hers normal.
When the girls put on their beautiful earrings
She doesn't put anything on her ears.
When we put on black shoes
She puts on brown shoes.

This is why we call her *Opposite!*

Varuni Ponniah (10)
Stanley Park Junior School

Now And Then Planets

P luto, blue, amazing, wonderful blue
L ittle solar systems all made up in one
A ir rockets flying through the discovering sky
N eptune, indigo-blue, I wonder if there's animals
E arth, sea, land and everything else,
  life is the only thing there
T ransport around these wonderful planets
  why, why can't I fly?
S aturn it is wonderful, space rings around its golden red globe.

Jessica Harris (10)
Stanley Park Junior School

Money

Money you spend
Pound notes you can bend
Money comes in silver, bronze and gold
You spend it when you're old
Pound notes come in red, purple and blue
You can spend it all on you!
Money you can buy books
Pound notes you can buy good looks.
Banks hold your money
So no need to worry!
Spend it on a car
Or on a drink in the bar.
Spend it on a beetle
Or on a pet eagle.
Spend money on some strawberry lips
Or on some lovely chips.
Spend it on a birthday cake
Or on a brand new rake.
Pound notes can buy you a new house
Or spend it on your cat's new toy mouse.

Jake Gray (11)
Stanley Park Junior School

Imagine

Imagine a giraffe as tiny as can be
then all of a sudden it turns taller as you can see.

Imagine a cheetah eating the grass
then all of a sudden it turns really fast.

Imagine a zebra as stripy as can be
stripy enough for me to ever see.

Imagine an ostrich as fast as can be
totally faster than me.

Imagine the cows fat and black
imagine them lazy and patched.

Imagine the antelope tough and rough
running fast without a puff.

Kiaran O'Leary (8)
Stanley Park Junior School

Imagine

Imagine a giraffe as slow as a tortoise
eating leaves from a tree.

Imagine a cheetah climbing a tree
and taking me.

Imagine a zebra galloping across the
smooth green grass.

Imagine an ostrich cantering proudly
as fast as a car.

Imagine the cows lazy and fat
grazing all the succulent grass.

Imagine the antelope galloping from
the terrible tiger.

Taha Maniar (9)
Stanley Park Junior School

Imagine

Imagine a giraffe as tall as a tree
eating some gold leaves and licking his nose.

Imagine a cheetah as fast as the wind,
showing its wrath on a tiny little calf.

Imagine a zebra so calm and bright
galloping elegantly against the wind and eating
the tall grass.

Imagine an ostrich as fast as the crashing waves
and charging gracefully on the brittle yellow grass.

Imagine the cows giving milk and lazily lying on the
dry ground eating the tall but yellow grass.

Imagine the antelope galloping from field to field,
running from the dreaded flesh eating cheetah.

William Maclachlan (9)
Stanley Park Junior School

Imagine

Imagine a giraffe as tall as could be
Then the next day she grows and waves
She's gone you can't even see.

Imagine a cheetah as speedy as can be
He's even too fast for me to see.

Imagine a zebra all black and white
He's really fast like the speed of light.

Imagine an ostrich as graceful as can be
If we raced he would definitely beat me.

Imagine the cows all eating the grass
They have such lovely fur it looks like brass.

Imagine the antelope all galloping past me
They are so speedy they are as fast as can be.

Martha Ketcher (8)
Stanley Park Junior School

On The Plain

On the plain
the stripy zebra grazes hungrily on the fresh green grass.

On the plain
the fast, vicious ostrich races gracefully across the dry,
brittle corn.

On the plain
the spotty camouflaged cheetah speeds happily across
the huge stretch of land.

On the plain
the long-necked giraffe munches quietly on the big juicy leaf.

On the plain
the lazy cow snores peacefully on the great green meadow.

On the plain
the sharp-horned antelope hunts silently for white petrified
mice.

On the plain
the slithery snake slides in the brown muddy field.

Ben James (8)
Stanley Park Junior School

A Recipe For A Good Book

First of all sprinkle a handful of romance,
Next add a tablespoon of action,
And a kilogram of horror.
Wait for a few minutes then
Add a gram of mystery.
Finally bake it for ten minutes
And . . . there it is,
A brilliant book!

Krishan Ganeshan (10)
Stanley Park Junior School

On The Plain

On the plain
the cunning cheetah dashes from side to side hungrily
looking for something to eat.

On the plain
the zebra gallops proudly across the gloomy grass.

On the plain
the python crawls slowly along, hissing at creatures and people.

On the plain
the birds fly happily past the sun while leaving their warm nest.

On the plain
the scared antelope runs fast when he spots the hungry cheetah.

On the plain
the tired tiger watches human flesh approaching her deep,
dark den.

Victoria Harding (8)
Stanley Park Junior School

Nature Is Safe

Misty skies following the wind
Birds looping in the air
Bears climbing trees searching for food
Wolves wearing their teeth out on a lump of meat
The hibernating squirrel curling up in a tight fisted ball
The natives coming to stop the polluting
and the killing of nature.

Sianna Lally (10)
Stanley Park Junior School

The World

Sacred sky
Beautiful birds
This is what it should look like.

Burning rubber
Tyres screeching
This is what it is like.

Gorgeous grasslands
Adorable fish
This is what we want.

Engines revving
Exhaust pipes puffing
This is what we've got.

Why is the world such a polluted place?

Alexander Maclachlan (11)
Stanley Park Junior School

England's Magic Number Nine

'Here he goes' says the commentator
'Round one defender, round another, he shoots! He scores.
Michael Smith really is England's magic number nine.'
Carried on the commentator.
'Michael stop daydreaming and answer the question'
Said the teacher.

Michael Short (10)
Stanley Park Junior School

Our World

Life is like a dream
A dream you can't explain
With forests green one day
The next all gone away
Rivers fresh and flowing
Next day green and ill.

People in the park like a happy family
Now full of teenagers doing lots of graffiti
Pollution is happening, happening all over the world
If we don't stop it soon all the wonderful things
Might just blow away
Be covered up by buildings
We don't need that much today.

So help try to stop pollution to help us every day
So people can get on in life in a happy way
Let's leave the world alone and just let it be
So everyone will get along quite joyfully.

Robyn Glover (10)
Stanley Park Junior School

The Sea

People snorkelling, watching fish
The fish swim, swivelling side to side
Jellyfish bob in the sea
The dolphins play far away with their silky skin
Seaweed floats on the top
Sandy salt floats on the rim of the sea
Waves crashing, turning, tumbling
The sandcastles get washed away
Shells in similar colour and shape
There is nothing like . . .
A day on the beach.

Francesca Bailey (10)
Stanley Park Junior School

Hot Or Cold Whatever The Weather

January, winter creeping over the corner,
February, glistening trees,
March, cold or hot whatever the weather
I don't know what,
April, leaves leap onto the floor as if they're alive,
May is a day for when we play,
June, the sun gleams out as if it's *summer!*
July, summer's here, hip hip hooray,
Come on everyone let's play,
August, summer's cooling down, oh no,
September, school starts, serious people everywhere
October, frozen people from top to bottom,
November, chilly fingers, frostbite on their toes,
December, *Christmas is here!*

Jessica Bourne (11)
Stanley Park Junior School

A Recipe For A Good Book

Take a pinch of horror
Add it to a bowl
Do this to have some fear and fill your mix with gore.
Add some love, just a tablespoon,
To give it a hint of romance too.
Give it a teaspoon of fighting
And give it some heroes and heroines.
Add some mystery and give it a blistering of ghouls,
That's enough to make the dough,
Now put it in the oven and get it tomorrow.
Then you have your perfect book
Now you can take it to school.

Naran Maistry (9)
Stanley Park Junior School

Anibet

A nts running through the grass
B ees bumping in the flowers
C ats licking their soft fur
D ogs running after a ball
E lephants gracefully walk rolling in mud
F ish glide through the weeds
G iraffes munching trees
H amsters nibbling nuts
I guanas' flaky skin
J aguar pouncing from tree to tree
K ing cobras slither in the grass
L ions roaring, *roar!*
M onkeys long tail entwined in the tree
N ewt blending in the water
O ctopus' eight legs ripple
P enguins swapping caring for their child
Q uails' wafer-thin skin
R ats' raggedy fur in the sewer
S nakes shedding skin after skin
T iger-orange and black fur soft as a baby's bum!
U nicorns gallop in a field
V ultures' razor-sharp eyes
W ater beetle under the deep blue sea
X tremely slow slug!
Y ellow tree frog, is it a leaf? No it's a frog!
Z ebra, he can't hide.

Amelia Hyatt (10)
Stanley Park Junior School

Fly

Fly, fly birdy, look out for gunmen in case you die.
If you see them
Fly away
And don't give up until
The end of the day.

And when you wake up
If the target you be
Fly again
Old man Trevor
Can't sit there forever.

George Fenner (11)
Stanley Park Junior School

Snake

Their skin has been shed
They gleam in the sun
And are ready to eat.

They see their prey
They stalk it with stealth
And are unseen in the grass.

Then they strike!
Snap! In go those venomous fangs
The rat it slowly dies.

The snake's jaw opens wide
The prey is gone
The snake has had his dinner
And is ready for night.

Karl Smith (10)
Stanley Park Junior School

Space

Gloomy, dark, nine planets, hot, cold, small, big.
Saturn has twelve moons.
Living things, martians, aliens, UFOs, they all could
be up there somewhere!
Aliens, big ones, small ones, heavy ones, light ones,
dark ones, bright ones.
Martians, kind ones, nasty ones, big spaceshipped ones,
small spaceshipped ones, big, small headed ones,
small, big bodied ones!
They all could be up there!

Max Harrison (11)
Stanley Park Junior School

Out Of This World

Aliens!
Short and fat
Thin and tall,
Spotted or striped,
Driving UFOs!
Round and square,
Flying saucers, spaceships,
Blue, red or green
Martians!
Green or orange,
Big or small,
Some strange, some normal,
Big headed or small headed,
They all live out of this world!

Stephen Rae (10)
Stanley Park Junior School

Seasons

Bouncing lambs,
Falling over,
Mothers lay asleep in a meadow.

Restless days,
Ten second nights,
Swimming pools wet once more.

Crunching leaves under your feet,
Getting colder
Wrap up warm.

Snowball fights,
Frosty nights
Children playing in the snow.

Laura Gardner (10)
Stanley Park Junior School

Summer

Winter's gone and summer's here
Now it's time to sing and cheer
Late night barbecues in the sun
Everybody's having fun.

Children have a race and swim
They all want to be the one to win
Parents sit and watch by the pool
Lying there and trying to be cool.

Friends enjoy the sun together
They hope they will always have this weather
It's great, there is sun,
It's lots of fun!

Gabriella Jeffery (11)
Stanley Park Junior School

Snowballs

S is for snow that lies on the ground
N is for nippy, that's winter for you
O is for only the *best* snowball fights
W is for water that freezes over
B is for birds to fly south for the winter
A is for altogether to have some fun
L is for locals to gather together
L is for lie-ins when the snow melts away
S is for *snowballs!*

Adam Russell (10)
Stanley Park Junior School

The Snow Journey

Icy snowflakes twirl
All around, settling gently
A shiny white blanket.

Slippery sliding snow
Snow folk dancing in the snow
Crunchy snow under foot.

Children are playing
Wrapped up warm with hat and scarf
Fingers red and raw.

Snowball fights begin
Gathering snow in our hands
Snow drips down our backs.

A snow angel made
A chilly experience
Excitement in the air.

The snow turns to slush
Children cry as snowmen melt
The snow fades away!

Stephanie Booth (11)
Stanley Park Junior School

Snow Is Here

Snow is here
Snow is there
Snow is everywhere!

The snow is glistening
When we're playing
Oh no, it's crumbling!

Snow is here
Snow is there
Snow is everywhere!

Throwing icy snowballs
At the frosted walls
Can you hear our calls?

Snow is here
Snow is there
Snow is everywhere!

The snow has started to melt
There will be no more snowballs to pelt
Ouch that one I felt!

The snow has come and been
There's no more to be seen
That I'm very keen.

Sophie Smith (10)
Stanley Park Junior School

Bunny

B ouncing, jumping, hopping around,
U nbelievably fast,
N othing to do just run, run, run,
N ow look what is coming,
Y um, yum, yum.

Laura Neal (11)
Stanley Park Junior School

Snow

I start my story
On a winter's day
The air is cold
The sky is grey.

The pretty white flakes
Start to fall from the sky
I look up above
And wonder why.

As it starts to settle
All on the ground,
Within a short time
It is all around.

As I start to walk
Leaving footprints in the snow
How are flakes made?
I've always wanted to know.

I just can't resist
To bend down and touch
The soft smooth snow
Oh I love it so much.

As the snow in my hands
Starts to melt away
Leaving icy cold water
It's a shame it can't stay.

For something so beautiful
For something so white
As the snow on the ground
Is like a bright shimmering light.

Oh how I love snow
Just wanted you to know!

Aimee Harwood (11)
Stanley Park Junior School

In The Snow Haikus

Snowballs in the air
Snow conceals the icy ground
Shall we play outside?

Freezing cold outdoors
Hands and feet are frozen hard
Oh how cold it is!

We're making snowmen
Rolling the snow on and on
Then breaking it up.

Now we've had enough
We're much too cold to stay here
We need to warm up.

James Jolley (11)
Stanley Park Junior School

What Is It?

Biting as a bat,
Nipping as a cat,
White as a Dalmatian,
Dense as a plantation,
What could that be?

Cold as a gale,
Compact as a snail,
Come on, let's have a go,
It's snow, snow, snow!

Chloe Robertson (11)
Stanley Park Junior School

Sprinkle A Bit Of This And That!

Get a spoonful of war
And put it in a bowl,
Then on top of that,
Put a handful of soul!

Into the mixture
Put a sparkle of horror,
Then leave it to rise all day till tomorrow!

When it's risen two inches,
Add a handful of romance,
Then grind it together,
With a whizz of entrance!

Put three cupfuls of trouble,
Into it all,
Then cover it up
And leave it to cool!

When it's cooled down
Mix a dash of frown,
Then add a gallon of glory,
And then mix it up with a little gory!

Put it into the oven,
And take it out,
So there's your wonderful story!

Eleanor Pryse-Hawkins (10)
Stanley Park Junior School

Untitled

Take a dash of horror and add a sprinkle of magic
Stir in a pinch of romance and a spoonful of humour
Add of course a touch of classic
Add a flash of reality and stir in it with milk
Put it in the oven for an hour or two
Take it out and sprinkle with a pinch of trouble.

That is my best book.

Frankie Wood (10)
Stanley Park Junior School

A Recipe For A Good Book

Get a bowl of humour with a pinch of adventure
Wait for an hour then put in a handful of pages
Wait for five minutes then put in a spoonful of fantasy.
Put in the oven for two hours.
Then get it out and sprinkle on some characters
> Now
> Your
> Book
> Is
> Done.

Charlotte Croucher (9)
Stanley Park Junior School

The Beach

When I walk along the beach
This is what I hear
Seagulls start to screech
People chatting on the pier.

Children laughing, swimming in the sea
People starting to go home
Adults on the sand having tea
But the children are starting to moan.

There are crabs running along the sand
Fish swimming in the sea
Children getting bitten on the hand
The fish are being taken home for tea.

Grace O'Leary (11)
Stanley Park Junior School

A Recipe For A Good Book

To start off with
You need a good sieve,
To get the lumps out of horror.
Now you can put your foot up until tomorrow.
When you've finished your rest
You've got to get the best of what you can find,
And give it a good grind
That's another load off your mind!
Now add a spot of humour and gore,
Then you're sure to find your perfect book.
All you have to do is take a look!

Ashley Luckyram (9)
Stanley Park Junior School

A Recipe For A Good Book

One bowl of horror
A gallon of gore
A handful of humour
Can we make some more?

A gram of silly events,
A spoonful of scariness
But try not to make a mess!

Two tablespoons of trifle
Then grill with some fighting
This recipe has got brilliant writing.

Lewis Farley (9)
Stanley Park Junior School

A Recipe For The Perfect Book

To make a perfect book . . .
Get a bowl and add a pinch of gore.
Chop up a gallon of love and sprinkle on top.
Get two tablespoons of mystery
Add a handful of adventure
And half a cup of reality.
Bake for half an hour.
Drizzle on an ounce of humour.
Don't forget a tablespoon of silly events.
Give it a whisk and a stir
But remember to ice on an interesting blurb.
Finally you will have a perfect book
So enjoy it and relax.

Amie Steele (10)
Stanley Park Junior School

Land, Sea, Air

L and animals scurrying along
A ggressive mammals, pouncing and leaping
N ans and family, all ancestors
D angerous lions.

S hocking sharks
E lectric eels
A nxious predators.

A tomic bombs flying through the air
I n their harrier jets and
R ed Barons.

Christopher Downing (10)
Stanley Park Junior School

A Recipe For A Book

First of all take a pound of gore
Then a tiny sprinkle of war.
A bowlful of classics and pour in some reality.
Put in a pinch of silly events and a smidge of scary fantasy.
In the bowl tip some mystery and adventure.
Take some funny language
And bake it together with some humour.
So now you've finished your recipe
And your story is a fantastic fantasy.

Cecily Snowball (10)
Stanley Park Junior School

Lion

Here comes the queen
Ready to pounce
On its prey
Running and jumping
Through the long beady grass
Its mane picking up all sorts of things
Don't look now, but she's caught her victim
And grabbed it around the neck.
    Down
        Down
            Down
                Sinks the gazelle.

Daniel Haines (11)
Stanley Park Junior School

A Recipe For A Good Book

A pinch of characters
And a teaspoon of love.
A big bowl of war
And a handful of gore.
Add a tablespoon of horror.
Chop up some adventure
And pour on some special effects.

Paul Staniforth (9)
Stanley Park Junior School

Paul And Me

I'm going
To Paul's for tea.
I feel excited
We're best friends
Paul and me.

He's kind.
He bought me pizza.
When he wants the telly
I want the PlayStation
And he doesn't mind.

He took me on holiday.
It only rained once.
We went to the market
And bought
Beyblades to play.

I'm going
To Paul's for tea.
We're best friends.
Next time
He can come to me.

David Hitchin (8)
The Mount Primary School

'Cat' In Sri Lanka

My cat doesn't have a name . . .
He's just 'Cat'.
He is sleeping on my toes
My toes feel warm
And my cat stays sleeping.

I take my cat
And put him on my pillow.
He miaows and then
Sleeps in a circle
Like a snake.

Outside the sun rises.
I get up and put my quilt
On the chair
And my cat
On the quilt.

I go outside
To brush my teeth.
The sun feels
So hot
On my body.

When I return
My cat is gone.
He will be walking . . .
Slowly . . .
On the white sand.

He comes home
At night
When the moon
And *thousands* of stars
Are in the sky.

Pragash Rasalingam (8)
The Mount Primary School

I Wish . . .

I wish that my dad was well
And we could travel
All the way around the world
Together.

I wish I could see my mum
Again . . .
That she would come alive
And bo with mo and my dad.

I wish that all the bad things
That have happened
Would
Go away.

I wish that all
My brothers
And sisters
Would make up.

I wish that
I could stay
At my school
Forever.

I wish that all
The flowers
Would grow
Again.

I wish
That it
Would
Snow.

Elizabeth O'Connell (9)
The Mount Primary School

Twinkles - The Hunting Cat

(Inspired by 'McCavity The Cat' by T S Eliot)

Twinkles is a Hunting Cat
She's called the Pouncing Paw.
For she's the mistress Hunting Cat
Who catches with her claws.

She's the bafflement of Ashcombe Square,
She's Mr Andy Hughes' despair,
For when he reaches the conservatory
Twinkles is not there.

Twinkles, Twinkles,
There's no cat like Twinkles.
Fluffy, silky, soft, adventurous
In a coat of silver sprinkles.

She's always got a mouse or two
To Andy Hughes' despair
But when he reaches the conservatory
Twinkles is not there.

Sian Hughes (8)
The Mount Primary School

Headache

I have a headache
His name is Thunder
He's like drum and bass
Bumpy, rough and heavy.
He's like a big, barking
Hair-raising boxer dog
And he starts silver
Then turns black.
He's like heavy machinery
Crashing and banging.
I need a steamroller to
Flatten him out.

Georgia Bailey (10)
The Mount Primary School

Snow

A snow sky is here,
Up there, high, not low.
The mouth of the wind opens
And lets out sparkles of snow.

I'll play on the slidey ice
And make snowballs
With my sister,
To throw at my brother . . . nice!

I'll walk on the snowy ground
And it will grab at my feet
And making groaning,
Crunching sounds.

There are thousands
Of diamonds all over the street
And they glitter
Although it is bitter.

Regina Khan (10)
The Mount Primary School

The Kitten Next Door

My neighbour next door
Has a newborn kitten,
He curls up on the floor
And he's lovely and warm.

He enjoys a cuddle
When he awakes
And he gets in a muddle
When he plays.

He licks your skin,
He tastes the salt
And out and in
Goes his tiny pink tongue.

Zoë Davis (8)
The Mount Primary School

The Sun

The sun glistens
Like a ball of fire in the sky.
Blindingly bright
It makes your eyes water and cry.

Hottest thing in the universe
It casts dark shadows that
Follow you around and
Make you feel brave.

It joins with the rain to make
A multicoloured rainbow
And reflects out of puddles
Looking like a sunflower.

Sam Besant (9)
The Mount Primary School

Barn Owl

I'm a big barn owl
I'm out on the prowl
Looking for vermin
Very determined.

From a great height
I give them a fright
I swoop down low
To have a good go.

The mouse is weak
I catch it in my beak
I've caught my prey
I'm proud to say.

Go back to my nest
To share it with the rest
The day is breaking
My babies are waking.

Bethany Russell (8)
The Mount Primary School

Dreams Of An Indian Dance

I am surrounded by space
I can zoom in or out
My music sounds sweet
It doesn't shout.
Dupatas waving as I move
Multicoloured
Like the setting sun
On the horizon.
Sari of silk and sequins
Twirling like a tornado
As I move
Spreading out like peacock feathers.
Bangles twinkling
High and low
As hands move
From head to toe.

Sakshi Kumar (11)
The Mount Primary School

Winter

Winter feels as cold as ice
I get a shiver down my spine
Like a *rush* of electricity.
Icicles hang from trees like bats
And the landscape looks
Like a white ocean.
Grass is covered with frost
Like putting gel on my hair.
No animals to see
Flowers are frozen and have died.
Winter is *much* too cold for me,
I can't wait until spring.

Daniel Halawi (11)
The Mount Primary School

Mind Blowing Street

The wind is thrashing in the trees
Noisy, abhorrent, ear-breaking.
Gigantic doors are slamming,
Glass is smashing,
Street lights are flickering.

Quicker than the mind
A huge, lanky figure stumbles past . . .
Blood is swimming.
Dogs are howling,
People are arguing,
The deep river is rushing and grabbing.

Thunder is breaking
Lightning is flashing
A creepy old gate creaks terribly.
Beautiful flowers, now dull,
And stinking are bending.
A killing fire is burning.

Aman Bajaj (11)
The Mount Primary School

The Lucky Traveller

The moonlight shone
In a cloak so white
Over deep green grass.
A traveller came
Through the shady darkness
When everyone else
Was asleep.
The traveller saw
A shiny sparkle,
Went to look
And found the glorious sight
Of diamonds!

Jason Pike (10)
The Mount Primary School

Remembrance

(Dedicated to Mr Tom Cox 1917-2004 - A fighter pilot in the Second World War)

Do you remember the brave soldiers?
What did they do?
What happened to them?
They saved me and you.
They went to Egypt and Italy too.

Do you remember the brave soldiers?
What did they see?
They saved you and me.
They saw pyramids and mummies
And gave their lives to put food in our tummies.

If they were not here,
What would we have done?
Some gave their lives by the hand of a gun.
Some came back to see their home
Others were buried all alone.

If they had not been here,
What would we do?
They saved me and you.
We will always remember you
Especially on Remembrance Day.

Loulse Thorne (10)
The Mount Primary School

The Butterfly

In a dull, dark room
It's all I want to look at,
The butterfly.

Unique and bright
It glides on soundless, silent wings,
And makes me smile.

I'm happy because
It's beautiful and looks like a rainbow,
The butterfly.

But sad because
It's so free,
And I'm stuck inside the house.

Its wings are
Thin and smooth
Like shiny paper.

In the garden
It picks the best flowers
To land on.

Kelly Neves (9)
The Mount Primary School

Volcano

Spitting, flaming, boiling hot, pouring lava,
Firing hot, the eruption has begun.
Burning crater, crackling flames,
Red-hot, sizzling terror, the eruption has begun.
Rocks falling down the slope,
Dust and ash in the air, the eruption has begun.
Crater cooling, lava slowing,
Turning solid, the eruption has ended.

James Tod (10)
The Raleigh School

Friends

Some friends are nice,
Some friends are bad,
Most friends are friendly,
But some are not.
Make sure you don't mix with the wrong kind,
Cos you'll come to a big surprise.

They'll only want you when your friends
Are not around.

People start to dislike you for who you play with,
It's not right for people to tell you what to do.
Being popular isn't everything,
I've mixed with the wrong kind,
I hope you don't!

Summer Dyason (11)
The Raleigh School

Hot Holidays

Holidays are great fun
No more school, just play in the sun
On holidays abroad meet new friends
Keep in touch and write letters to send
Go by boat or catch the train
Travel by car or take off by plane
Places to visit near or far
Caravans, tents or hotels 5-star
Take your pick and leave your worries behind
Have a great time, relax and unwind
Sun, sea and sand is everywhere to see
It's a wonderful place for children to be!

Daryl Thompson (10)
The Raleigh School

A Lonely Life

A cold and miserable life, someone who keeps things
To themselves.

Can't tell anyone about anything,
They keep it in so long it just comes out as nothing.

In the playground no friends, sitting by yourself,
You don't have anyone to talk to.

As the day goes on you just get lonelier and lonelier and can't stop it,
It's like a roller coaster - you can't control it.

You feel lonely and sad, nothing can make it feel better,
When you try to tell someone, it just comes out as nothing.

There you are ten years later and you've got a smile on your face,
You're with your friends - this is a life you love to have.

Louise Auld (11)
The Raleigh School

The Earthquake

The night was soft and quiet,
I was wrapped up in my bed,
Then I heard a rumbling noise,
I thought it was in my head.

My bed began to shudder,
All my books fell on the floor,
The windows began to rattle,
As I quickly shot out of the door.

The oak tree came tumbling down,
I gasped and started to scream,
I woke up in a fright
And realized it was just a dream!

Megan Cook (9)
The Raleigh School

Christmas Memories

Christmas has gone,
The tree has gone and the tinsel has gone,
But the presents are here,
Even though I *was* a naughty boy on Christmas Day.

First I overfed the cats,
They were sick all over the sitting room floor,
Just as Father Christmas came through the door.
I had my slingshot in my hand,
Ready to fire the angel off the tree,
When Father Christmas shouted,
'Oi! Don't shoot that angel off the tree,
Or you'll get no presents from me.'
The shot slung out,
It hit Father Christmas on the head,
'Oh my gosh, I think he's dead!'

But no,
He was just bruised instead.
I didn't hang around,
I didn't stand my ground,
I simply ran away.
'Oh dear, I think I've blown it,
I don't think he'll come next year,
Maybe he'll forgive me,
After all it is the season of good cheer.'

The funny thing was that Daddy appeared at breakfast time
With a large plaster on his forehead,
So he spent the rest of the day asleep in bed.
Merry Christmas!

David Spratt (10)
The Raleigh School

Woolacombe Bay

I'm on my way to Woolacombe Bay
And all I can say is 'Hooray!'
When you arrive
In the stunning blue swimming pool,
When you go to the beach
You can wash your feet
In the big, wonderful sea.
It's lovely and hot,
It's not cold and rot,
Oh, your head's always filled with glee.
And the food is awfully nice,
You get lovely pizza,
Or fish or rice.
You can play ping-pong or pool,
Or neither at all.
When it's time to leave,
You don't want to go,
But it's good to know
You can always go back next year!

Sam Holman-Hirst (10)
The Raleigh School

The Kitchen

The kitchen is a nice place
It's full of lovely treats
But when it comes to savoury
No one wants to eat.
My mum says, 'It's healthy.'
I really don't agree,
I wouldn't eat a single bit
If it weren't for pocket money.
When it comes to pudding,
We're all sitting in our chairs.
We're waiting for our mum
To bring us some chocolate eclairs!

Elin Keyser (9)
The Raleigh School

What Are Little Girls . . .

I'm not a sugar and spice girl
An all things nice girl
A do-as-told
Good as gold
Pretty frock
Never shock
Girl.

I'm a slugs and snails girl
A puppy dogs' tails' girl
A climbing trees
Dirty knees
Hole in sock
Love to shock
Girl.

Cricket bats
And big, white rats
Crested newts
And football boots

That's what this little girl's . . .
Made of!

Gemma Fraser (11)
The Raleigh School

A Christmas Wish

Today is the day for presents and joy,
To remember the birth of a special boy,
Eat turkey, trimmings and Christmas pud,
But remember to stop eating when you think you should.
The day is nearly finished and everything has gone well,
But St Nicholas is already preparing for another Christmas Noel.

James Fox (10)
The Raleigh School

My Cat Called Seesaw

I have a cat called Seesaw
This is the story of his nine lives.

Numbor ono: got burnt by the sun.
Number two: fell in the loo.
Number three: dropped out of a tree.
Number four: got stuck in the door.
Number five: got caught in a beehive.
Number six: got squashed by sticks.
Number seven: was driven to Devon (had to walk back).
Number eight: was stepped on by Kate.

He hasn't used up life number nine
And he's just fine.
(And I still love him!)

Catherine Johnston (9)
The Raleigh School

Lord Of The Rings

All my family are Lord of the Rings mad.
My brother, my mum and don't forget my dad.
I've been to see the films lots of times,
The girls would say Aragorn is so divine.

I've seen it with my friends and my cousins,
I've got mini figures, dozens and dozens.
I've got a lunch box with Legolas on
And on my bed I've got Gimli stuck on.

Men are good and Orcs are bad,
The evil eye of Sauron rules the land.
The vast spreading army takes everything it touches,
It will soon be in the Dark Lord's clutches.

Into Mordor where shadows lie,
Into Mordor where Orcs will die.

Connor O'Hara (10)
The Raleigh School

Noise!

Hoovers, alarm clocks, loud music too,
Cars screeching, dogs barking, flushing of loos.

Noise!

Babies are crying and shouting out loud,
Banging from doors and noise from the crowd.

Noise!

Old gates creaking, smoke alarms beeping,
Motors of aeroplanes, road workers drilling.

Noise!

Ambulances ringing towards a rugby match,
Jonny Wilkinson broke his leg by trying to catch.

Noise!

Sunshine, green grass and birds singing high,
Butterflies fly and no sight of cry.

Peace!

Lucas de Carvalho (10)
The Raleigh School

Friends

Friends are forever
Friends are for you
Friends can help you
When you're feeling blue
No matter what you do
They will still be there for you.

Andrea Gould (9)
The Raleigh School

Safari Animals

Elephants are big and grey,
They also like to bath and play.
They use their trunks to spray their back
And also like to paint in black.

Lions sleep then prowl around,
Until a tasty meal is found.
They race the vultures to the prey
And tear it up in a horrible way.

Now giraffes are tallest on the land,
They eat the leaves but not with hands.
They stretch their necks up to the sky
And curl their tongues round leaves up high.

Jaguars stand proud and strong,
Some of their tails are very long.
The only food that jaguars eat
Are very big portions of meat.

Now what is this that I have found?
A great big hippo buried in the ground.
He wallows around in his own little way,
He hasn't done much for most of the day.

In Africa on the grassland plain,
Where it hardly ever rains,
All these creatures you can see,
If you're lucky to go on safari!

Rebecca Evans (10)
The Raleigh School

The Burp

Oh my goodness, here it comes
A little burp rising from my tum
Any minute, any moment of any day
This little burp can come out to play.

It's something that I really hate
But It's usually because of what I ate
And goodness, I feel such a fool
When it happens at school!

How embarrassing, how shocking it is for me
When this little burp comes up to set itself free!
All my classmates turn around
So does my teacher when she hears its sound.

The girls and boys laugh out aloud
Miss D looks black at me, like a thunder cloud
No more little burps in class anymore
If I want to pass my exams, to be sure!

Megan Lane (9)
The Raleigh School

Primates

Primates come in all sizes and shapes
There are orang-utans, gorillas, chimps and apes

Primates eat bananas, aphids and fruits
But you'd better watch out 'cause they can be brutes

The chimpanzee is my favorite one
He's cute, he's active, he's handsome and fun

I'm sure you've seen chimps drinking tea at a table
Opposable thumbs are what makes them able

There's one other primate that I really like too
Can you guess which it is?
You should, it's you!

Robert Allott (11)
The Raleigh School

Autumn

Orange golden leaves
Falling, twirling to the ground
Under the trees
Making a carpet of leaves
Leaves are dancing
Falling all around us
All the leaves are dry and crunchy
It gets cold and misty
Birds fly away to
Hotter places
I love autumn.

Kate Nicholls (7)
The Raleigh School

The Stars And The Moon

I sit up in bed and gaze at the stars
They're smiling back at me.
I think of happy things,
Not sad.
I think of good things,
Not bad.

The moon is as white as a pearl
And as round as a ring.
The sky is as black as a hole.
I think of happy things,
Not sad.
I think of good things,
Not bad.

Then I fall quickly off to sleep.
Zzzzzzzzzz . . .

Hannah Punshon (10)
The Raleigh School

The English Country

There is a small country called England,
Quite mild is this place.
One day is cold and horrible,
Next is sunny and hot.

People on the beach,
Sitting on some towels,
Some in the sea splashing around
Or having a donkey ride.

Weekends in the country,
Amongst the sheep and cows.
People think it's boring
But it's a real surprise!

Walking through the city,
Amongst the clustered clouds.
Only polluted air to breathe
And rubbish on the ground.

All in all England's great,
In every single way.
From take-aways
To five-course meals
And parks to play footie in!

Nicholas Edwards (11)
The Raleigh School

My Cat

I love to watch my cat
He does many interesting things
I'd like to have a chat
About if he'd like some wings
I'm sure he would say yes
'Cause he loves to be high in trees
Wings would keep him out the mess
He'd be free of mud and fleas!

Kate Penny (10)
The Raleigh School

Water

Water is a killer,
But also keeps us alive.
It drowns us and we drink it,
How can we possibly survive?

It kills people in Bangladesh,
And wrecks their homes too.
Bangladesh has lots of it,
But Africa needs it too.

Africa, a barren land,
Needing lots of water.
People washing, drinking too
And making bricks and mortar.

Douglas Hampshire (10)
The Raleigh School

Transport

Down in the underground there are lots of trains,
The vandals go there to cut the mains.

Up in the air there are lots of planes,
They fly fifty times higher than average cranes.

So get on the motorway, drive as you may,
You might find you'll be there another day.

Down on the driving range, Tiger gets par,
While on the racetrack, Schumacher's in his car.

Dylan Brychta (11)
The Raleigh School

I Like Football

Football is my favorite sport
People can play it from tall to short
The object of the game is to score a goal
In the two halves that make a whole
Try not to cause a foul
Especially not to your pal
You need to be prepared to get muddy
Try and pass to your buddy
It doesn't matter if you play in the rain
You need to say 'I will win the game.'

Robbie Kenny (10)
The Raleigh School

The Bridge

I am lonely, a bridge made of stone,
There's no one around but I shall not moan.
And for years I have stood,
Deep in the wood,
No one showed
And the river still flowed.
I have learnt many a thing,
Yet for the first time I began to sing.
I felt great, I felt sad, I felt found, I felt lost,
I could not run, I could not hide.
And this was the cost,
The birds flew around,
Without a sound,
They were so confused,
I was almost moved.

Katie Fuller (10)
The Raleigh School

The Black Briefcase

We had to go there in the car
Although it wasn't very far
I was nervous, Mum was too
I knew exactly what I had to do
We parked and looking, saw a face
Fierce with glasses and black briefcase
We followed him with terror and fear
Knowing my fate was near
At least there was one friendly smile
I went alone with her for a while
Left poor Mum contemplating my fate
She tried to sew but couldn't concentrate
I finally entered the testing room
Saw the briefcase and filled with gloom
I waited for the trial to start
Aware of my rapidly beating heart
I tried my best as I knew I should
After a false start it all came good
When I emerged I even managed a smile
And Mum looked relieved after a short while
We went home then to tell my dad
Grade two flute hadn't been that bad.

Emily de Beaux (11)
The Raleigh School

Robin Hood

Robin Hood, Robin Hood, he was brave,
He stole from the rich and to the poor he gave.
Robin Hood, Robin Hood, he gave to us when we were poor
And we didn't have enough,
Robin Hood, Robin Hood, be with us now,
For what can we do without you - and how?

Eleanor Johnston (8)
The Raleigh School

War Poem

When war is started
We're usually parted
But who can see the sense in war?
Why do we always want more?
Why not be happy with what we've got?
Why let country and people rot
While we fight for more
And maybe start a Third World War?
We let hundreds of soldiers die
As the years of war go by
We let hundreds of people starve and get ill
At our own will
Because when war is started
We're usually parted.

Kimberley Jarvis (11)
The Raleigh School

The Colosseum

I walk past the Colosseum
And see its wonderful sights,
I think that I was there in the past,
Included in all the battles and fights.
A sword by my side
And a helmet on my head,
I really, really wish,
That I was at home in bed.
The Emperor stares at me,
I cannot give up now,
I must foresee my victory,
To make my family proud.
I think about this every day,
Each time I walk by,
The grand Colosseum in Rome,
It sometimes makes me cry.

Catherine Roberts (10)
The Raleigh School

Shark!

King of the seas this eating machine,
It eats any fish in its way.
There are loads of different types in the sea,
But don't get in any shark's way,
For it'll charge for you,
Mouth wide open, teeth bared, designed to kill.
But it's not likely it'll eat you up,
For there is only one man-eating type of shark,
The Great White,
The king of all killing machines.
It eats seals and surfers!
But before you tremble with fear,
The attacks are rare
And happen hundreds of miles away.
But beware, sharks are living in the sea
And next time you meet one,
It'll chomp you!

Olivia Flaherty (10)
The Raleigh School

A Rhyme About My Friends

Jamie is always nice
Samuel is always eating rice.

Niall is always in bed
Kyra likes to cuddle her ted.

Victoria is my friend
Emily drives me round the bend.

Dominic likes to play football
Matthew G is very tall.

All of us are very good friends
And that is how the story ends.

Howard Jennings (7)
The Raleigh School

Sleeping Beauty

Once upon a time
In the land of rhyme
Lived a queen desperate for a kid
Finally she won a baby girl on an Internet bid
The queen had a celebration
All the fairies had an invitation
The fairies gave gifts of beauty and love
Then there was a loud *boom* from up above
With a huff and a puff and a bang of smoke
In came the dark fairy with a long purple cloak
'How dare you forget me!
I'll give you a present for your kiddie!
When she's sixteen
She'll walk in the door that she's never seen
She'll walk in the door
And prick her finger
And fall on the floor!'
Sixteen years later she then found a door
She had never seen before
She then pricked her finger and fell on the floor!
One hundred years later
A prince rode by
He went in the castle
And gave a sigh
As he saw the princess who there did lie
'Oh no, she's not pretty
Her teeth are gritty
Her hair is nitty
All that way for nothing!'

Stephanie Rendall (11)
The Raleigh School

Swimming In Paradise

I love swimming,
With the waves lapping by your side,
It feels lovely being weightless,
Like a feather.
It is like being in a cloud,
Surrounded by dreams,
Nothing in the world to bother me,
Nothing to ever go wrong.
No instructions to tell you what to do,
You are in the driving seat,
You are in control,
The waves are working for you.
Dancing in the pool,
Feeling the water surround you, swallowing you up,
A wonderful sensation.
But when you get out,
You have to part with paradise,
Until next time.
We shall have fun,
When child meets with water,
Once you are back on this planet,
You shall dance again
In the watery waves.

Louise Patterson (10)
The Raleigh School

Fire

Fire, fire, it burns so bright
Fire, fire, warm, warm delight
Toasting crumpets on a stick
With butter so very thick
The embers glowing in the dark
Was once a tree with thick bark
Fire still is glowing red
Come on now, off to bed!

Jennifer Stonely (11)
The Raleigh School

The Day I Saw A Pirate

One day I saw a pirate,
A real one out at sea,
He took his shaggy hat off
And waved it twice at me.

He flashed his sword to show it off
And cut off a ship rat's head,
He couldn't make out why it didn't move,
'Til he realized it was dead.

Then a big ship came up behind him,
Driven by a deadly pirate called Boss,
The pirate didn't know what to do,
He was totally at a loss.

Boss shot at him and missed,
Then again and again and again,
Boss was so frustrated with his gun,
That he couldn't feel the pain.

The pirate had shot his bare left knee
And Boss collapsed on his deck,
Then the pirate's parrot flew at him
And gave him a well earned peck.

The pirate then looked back at me
And gave me a cheery grin,
Then his parrot flew right back to me
And dropped something on my chin.

A little golden ring,
So I can remember him forever,
And I won't forget him, no I won't,
Not never, never, never.

Malin Stensson (11)
The Raleigh School

Chelsea

Hey, hey,
Wherever you may be,
We are the famous CFC.
Go to Stamford Bridge and you will see,
Chelsea manager, Claudio Ranieri.
If you like footy, see The Blues,
They're so good, they're always in the news.
Get your ticket online or from a tout,
Sit in your seat and let us hear you shout.
All our team will show you our might,
For the opposition, arriverderci, goodnight.
For next season it might be Sven,
But then there's always chairman Ken.
By next Christmas we could be very, very merry,
Hopefully our defence won't be as soft as a cherry.
Join The Blues, you won't regret it,
Next thing you know you'll be wearing our kit.

Oliver Carpenter (11)
The Raleigh School

Tennis

Tennis is my favourite sport,
When playing on a gravel court,
To hit the ball over the net,
Requires quite a lot of sweat.

To make the opponent go off course,
You've got to make him a little hoarse,
To do the quite amazing feat,
You've got to get a swinging beat.

Jonathan Nicholas (10)
The Raleigh School

Dogs

You've just come out,
You can't open your eyes,
The gigantic world,
Is a huge surprise.

It's your first time outside,
With this green, stringy stuff,
There's so much to do,
You just can't get enough.

Oh, I'm so lucky,
To be a puppy.

Sarah Owens (10)
The Raleigh School

Fairy Footprints

Fairy footprints everywhere,
Big ones, small ones,
Fairy footprints.
Fairy footprints in the house,
On the carpet, everywhere,
Fairy footprints.
Fairy footprints along the wall,
Down the hall,
Fairy footprints.
Fairy footprints everywhere,
Big ones, small ones,
Fairy footprints.

Lydia Charteris-Black (9)
The Raleigh School

Gazelle

The graceful gazelle
Is a marvellous creature,
Because each one
Has a distinguished feature.

The graceful gazelle
Is stupendous,
Because it is calm,
That's just one feature.

The graceful gazelle
Is an outstanding creature,
Because the older the gazelle,
The more of a teacher
And that's just two features.

The graceful gazelle
Is a fab creature,
Because out of all that could be,
The gazelle is one thing that you cannot see.

Hallam Breen (8)
The Raleigh School

The Dodo

Did you ever wonder if the dodo was true?
Do you think they lived wild or in a zoo?
Do you think they were colourful birds
Or do you think they had funny beaks and looked like nerds?
There are so many questions to answer and so little time.
I think they were very innocent birds.
I don't think they did a crime.

Kelly Brychta (9)
The Raleigh School

The Invisible Beast

The invisible beast is stalking around,
Through the trees and rocky ground.

The monster leaves a slimy trail,
A bit like a slug or a snail.

His hair is fiery, bloodshot red,
He would scare a man half dead.

His skin is squelchy, slimy green,
He really is never clean.

He moans all day until the day is out,
And then he starts to yell and shout.

In the morning the beast walks through a sunlit path,
'Hmmm . . . for breakfast I shall have a nice juicy calf.'

Though you cannot see him and if you want to know why,
The truth is he is rather shy.

He hides in the woods until the moon is high,
Then he comes out to seek his prey,
That greedy thing,
He eats all day!

Dominic Barnes (9)
The Raleigh School

Trees

I have seen trees,
They wave in the breeze.
Their trunks are tall,
Their leaves are small.
They flutter in the air,
Their leaves are like hair.
I have seen trees,
They wave in the breeze.

Emma Crighton (9)
The Raleigh School

Noises

The car coming up the drive,
Crunch, crunch, crunch.

A caterpillar eating,
Munch, munch, munch.

I hear a chick going
Cheep, cheep, cheep.

Then I hear a car going
Beep, beep, beep.

I hear the windmill going
Round and round.

I hear someone walking on the
Leaves on the ground.

If you listen with your ears,
There are lots of things you will hear.

Grace Cochran (10)
The Raleigh School

Fish In A Tank

My friend keeps fish in a tank
One's called Stripe, one's called Frank
One's called Tiger, one's called Dot
The other one has a great big spot
They don't do much but swim around
I think she bought the lot for one pound.

Matthew Penny (8)
The Raleigh School

The World Of The Deep

My dear darkness, the deep blue,
To you I shall return.
What secrets lie in the wondrous beyond?
Your mysteries carry on the waves.
I wonder, in the depth, what magic lurks,
As I hear the whispers of the foam.
The songs of your world echo from under your vast surface,
Why is your world so different from mine?

Natalie Holroyd (10)
The Raleigh School

No Messin'

No messin', we must win by a
Big margin, we need a vitamin!

Hockey, you must score once or
Twice, break the ice, or else you
Will pay the price.

Lure crowds to the rink,
Get a hot dog and a drink.

No messin', we must win by a
Big margin, we need a vitamin!

Football gets the adrenalin
Pumping, players here, there,
Tackling, jumping.

Let's win the Superbowl,
Who will play the starring role?

Niall Wright (9)
The Raleigh School

My Family

My family is big
But some members are small
If we put everyone together
We would have to have a large hall!

I have lots of cousins
Aunts and uncles too
Sometimes it is difficult to tell
Who belongs to who!

My relatives live all around the world
England, Iran, America, Germany and Spain
My mum's brother likes to live in a hot country
And where he lives there is very little rain!

Yasmin Beckett (10)
The Raleigh School

Vesuvius

A low rumble in the mountain,
Like an old man's grumble,
Then a big explosion
And the crater spat out,
Burning fire followed by sizzling hot rocks.
The lava started flowing
Like a slow trickle of blood
And picked up speed
As it bolted down the mountain,
Destroying everything in its path.
Vesuvius had no respect for the people and homes in Pompeii,
Weeks later when Vesuvius' danger had died down,
Destruction was seen in grey ash   ·
And the mountain was quiet once again.

Marcus Gilbert (9)
The Raleigh School

Football Crazy

I'm football crazy
Like my mum and dad
My dad's so football crazy
He plays it with his apples
My mum's so football crazy
She plays it with a can
And me, I'll play it with anything
Even a round frying pan
And my brother is such a football whizz
I bet you couldn't beat him
Anyway I wouldn't care if you did
And my friend Jamie, he does it all the time
He kicks the ball like crazy
Even in the classroom
When everybody's working
You can see him there kicking his legs
Now over to my friend Samuel
He does it too
He plays it in the garden
So do I too.

Niall O'Hara (8)
The Raleigh School

I Like . . .

I like chocolate because it is nice
Instead of eating rice.
I like chips
And don't forget the fish.
I like bacon with a roll
Or sometimes with an egg as well.
But I like sausages
Best of all.

Dominic Carpenter (7)
The Raleigh School

Winnie The Pooh And Friends

Winnie the Pooh is happy,
Winnie the Pooh is fun,
Winnie the Pooh is scatty,
He has a great big tum!

Piglet is little,
Piglet is sweet,
Piglet is caring,
He has tiny feet!

Tigger is bouncy,
Tigger is big,
Tigger is pouncy,
Tigger likes to jig!

Eeyore is gloomy,
Eeyore is glum,
Eeyore is a slow walker,
He doesn't ever have fun!

Rabbit is rude,
Rabbit is cross,
Rabbit is a chatterbox
And thinks he is the boss!

Owl is brainy,
Owl is wise,
Owl is magic,
He never walks, he flies!

Victoria Holloway (7)
The Raleigh School

Going To The Cinema

We're going to the cinema, just you, my mum and me,
We're going to have lots of delicious popcorn,
Two bags of sweets, one for you and one for me,
We're going to sit on big, comfy seats,
Oh, we're going to the cinema, oh, what a treat.

We're going to watch a movie, on a wide screen,
We're going to watch a new movie, which we haven't seen,
We're going to eat our yummy popcorn and bags of sweets,
We're going to the cinema, just you, my mum and me.

Christie Dowling (7)
The Raleigh School

My Baby Twins

My twins are cute,
My twins are sleepy,
Sometimes they are good
And sometimes they are whiney.
Four hands, four feet,
Sometimes naughty, sometimes sweet.
Four eyes, four ears,
Sometimes happy, sometimes tears.
Teddy bears make them smile,
Then they might cry for a while.
Maybe tired, maybe hungry,
Or they may want a cuddle with me.
Twenty fingers, twenty toes,
But each twin has one nose.
They pull funny faces, then they rest,
My baby twins are just the best.

Verity Barnes (8)
The Raleigh School

The Beach

The other day I went to the beach,
Stuck my toe in the water and boy did I screech.
I felt that my body was starting to freeze,
It crept up my leg and into my knees.

I stepped out of the water and back onto land,
Then something mysterious came out of the sand.
It was a huge crab, it was coming for me,
So I turned around quickly and jumped back into the sea.

I swam so far that a current took me,
I wished that I'd brought my favourite teddy.
I started to get a very cold head,
I wished that I was tucked up in bed.

I saw something swimming around with some kelp,
It was a dolphin calling for help.
I was sinking fast and I started to scream,
And then I woke up, it was only a dream.

Sophie Brindle (9)
The Raleigh School

My Rabbit Has Got This Habit

I've got this rabbit
And it's got this habit,
I go out of my room, then come back in
And suddenly *boom!*
It's pooped all over the place
And look at Mum's face!
So I take my rabbit outside,
Then have a go on the slide,
After I put it in the hutch,
But it never eats much,
So I give it a treat
And then I start to get sore feet,
I was the one who had to clear up all the mess,
Oh, what a distress!

Jessica Richardson (10)
The Raleigh School

The Apocalypse

When the day turns dark,
You know it has come.
When time stops,
You know it has come.
When there's fear everywhere,
You know it has come.
When shadows are everywhere,
You know it has come.
When there is no happiness left,
You know it has come.
When hope ceases to exist,
You know it has come.
When there are no good memories left,
You know it has come.
When there's nothing to do,
You know it has come.
When things don't matter anymore,
You know it has come.
When there's nothing left . . .

Alexander Eller (9)
The Raleigh School

My Friend

She's special and loyal and great company,
Chatty, helpful and means a lot to me.
She never is mean to me,
Whatever I do,
She is always there for me,
The whole day through.
Her name is . . . ?

Clare Strange (9)
The Raleigh School

On The Fields Of Flanders

On the fields of Flanders
A bullet goes passing by
The man beside you shouts,
'Why do we fight? Why?'
Then he falls down dead,
His hand still in the sky,
On the fields of Flanders,
Death is coming nigh.
On the fields of Flanders,
A Frenchman dies,
And there a poppy grew,
Bright, beautiful, tall and new.
On the fields of Flanders,
A Frenchman lies.

Christopher Hinchliff (10)
The Raleigh School

My Favourite Friend

My name is Zoe Light
And I have a pony called Flight.

He loves to run across the plains,
So I need to have a good grip on his reins.

His colour is grey
And I just wanted to say . . .

He is my pony and I love him.

Zoe Light (10)
The Raleigh School

Swimming

Swimming at Wey Valley is my hobby,
I work so hard, my muscles get wobbly.
When I'm racing, my family cheer,
Louder than anyone, my grandma I hear!

The toughest stroke is butterfly,
It makes my arms ache till I want to cry!
You lift your arms up to the sky,
When you breathe you see them whizzing by.

Breaststroke makes me feel like a frog,
But it is as easy as a little jog.
You kick your legs out wide and strong,
Then you make them nice and long.

The most enjoyable of them all,
Is when I do the front crawl.
It is really fast, strong and quick,
I like it because I am long and slick.

With backstroke I look to the sky,
I don't like it, I'll tell you why:
Swimming along the water goes,
Across my face and up my nose.

Charlie Powell (10)
The Raleigh School

Bullying

My head hurts,
My ear aches,
As I pull in with a squeal of my brakes.
It's the constant bullying
Makes me tired.
Teachers!
They should all be fired.

Adam Knox (10)
The Raleigh School

Holidays

Holidays are really good,
For swimming in the sea
Slurping down that mint ice cream
That's the holiday for me!

Holidays beside the pool
Are supposed to be with rest,
Sunbathing in a white deckchair
For Mum, they are the best!

Holidays upon the course
Are really golf for Dad!
But for us the secret is,
They're actually really bad!

Holidays in the rain,
Are completely, utterly glum
But for the quackie duckies
They're excellent fun!

Ailsa Keyser (9)
The Raleigh School

My Pet Spider

I have a pet spider, his name is Sam
He lives in a shoebox next to my bed
He has eight little shoes and one warm hat
He scares all the teachers and the kids too
But one day he was making a cobweb
And guess what, it was on the teacher's chair
This is really sad, you don't want to hear
The teacher sat on him!

Sonia Smith (9)
The Raleigh School

My Best Friend

She was my best friend,
She isn't anymore.
We did everything together,
We've never fought before.

A new girl joined our class,
She seemed quite nice at first.
Then she caused some trouble,
The way she did it you would think she'd rehearsed.

I have no idea why,
But she hung around with us.
I knew she'd come in-between my friend and I,
So I started to make a fuss.

My friend got really annoyed with me
And she left me on my own.
She never ever talks to me now,
She hangs up when I phone.

Kiran Desor (10)
The Raleigh School

The Chef In The Restaurant

There once was a chef with a very tall hat,
He worked in a restaurant with a very small cat.
His favorite dish was a plate of spaghetti
And he'd cry, 'Mama mia,' to his wife, Betty,
Who would serve their guests with a smile and a wink,
And if you were careful and didn't blink,
You might also see the cat did too!

Daniel de Carvalho (8)
The Raleigh School

My Twin

When I was born I was not alone
But I didn't mind, I didn't moan
Out of Mummy's tummy along with me
Came my twin sister, Meggie.

'Aren't they alike' people have always said
These are the words that I really dread
I am Harriet and I am mo
She is Meggie and she is she!

So everyone, take a close look please
You can tell us apart with ease,
She has a mole on her left cheek
I am the one that's mild and meek.

The confusion drives me totally mad
And sometimes even makes me sad
You see, my face is oval, her face is round
My voice is high and hers has a deep sound!

It's nice to have a sister, for sure
I really couldn't ask for more
But it really causes so much trouble
Because everyone sees her as my double!

Harriet Lane (9)
The Raleigh School

Teddy Bears

Teddy bears are cuddly
Teddy bears are sweet
Teddy bears are what
You go to bed with
And cuddle when you sleep.

Teddy bears are scary
Teddy bears are hairy
Teddy bear's best friend
Is a fairy.

Rebekah Lock (9)
The Raleigh School

Snowman

With the snow
We had this year,
We made a snowman,
He filled me with fear.

He was tall as Mum,
Wide as Dad,
It was easy to make him,
With the snow we had.

He had flippers for feet,
A carrot for a nose,
Screwdrivers for eyes
And pebbles for toes.

He towered over us all,
We felt really small,
But now he is dead,
All that's left of his head . . .

Is nothing!

Anna Flight (10)
The Raleigh School

Winter Weather

The weather outside is frightful,
The weather ain't so delightful,
Why can't it be snow?
I really don't know,
It's always rain,
I think I might go insane.

Vanessa Rand (9)
The Raleigh School

People Around Me!

Hoorah, it's the weekend,
Time to have fun and play,
'But not forgetting the homework,'
So our teachers say.

So what shall I do today?
I'll have a look at the weather,
To decide where I should play,
But what will my parents say?

I have made up my mind,
'Yippee,' my parents say,
So it's off to play in the garden,
'Don't get too cold,' Mum shouts!

What's going to happen today?
Dad says, 'Are you ready for rugby?'
'Of course I'm ready,' I reply.
'Time for a warm-up, boys,' shouts the coach.

Sam Maycock (9)
The Raleigh School

My Giraffe

My giraffe is tall and straight,
My giraffe is looking for a mate.
It comes from Africa I know,
My giraffe can bend down low
And drinks from the river's flow.
With his eye so high,
He can see the clouds in the sky.
With a coat of brown and yellow
And his neck so long I know.
His four stilt-like legs
Will get ready to go.
My giraffe is the best I know.

Emily Stanford (8)
The Raleigh School

Hair

Hair, hair, everywhere,
On your nose,
Under your chair.

In the bathroom,
In the sink,
On your eyelashes when you blink.

Hair on your armpits,
Hair on your chest,
Some people use it as a vest,
Or some people dye it *pink!*

Now some people haven't got any hair . . .
They are bare!

The hair that's on your chin,
The hair that's on your head,
All seems to fall off
And make you itch in bed.

Oh, all of the hair,
Where does it come from?
It's not fair!
But what is *hair?*

Lewis Robinson (9)
The Raleigh School

My Dog

My dog plays ball with me,
My dog comes for a walk with me,
We play in the fields,
We look for badgers in the ground.
She is an English bull terrier,
She is so kind,
Her name is Tess
And we all think she's the best!

Hetty Davies (9)
The Raleigh School

I Love Lego

Lego, Lego, I love Lego,
I love building Lego.
In my bedroom, down the stairs,
I build Lego near and far.
I build streets, roads,
Skyscrapers and a Ferrari car.
My brother loves Lego,
He is building the Legy Cauldron bar.
My mum hates Lego because it makes lots of mess.
Boxes of Lego, models.
Dusting everywhere, it makes her tear her hair.
I got a Red Baron for Christmas,
Making it every day,
Playing with it in my spare time,
That makes a rhyme for Christmas time, hey!

Joshua Tolley (9)
The Raleigh School

Orbiting

The space place, the moon race,
With plenty of planets to see,
Like Saturn with rings,
But I've got plenty of those things,
Or maybe Pluto, like a tiny ball.
I'm hungry now,
Is the moon made of cheese?
If it was I'd be pleased.
What's over there that is so bright?
It's dissolving the night.
It must be a star,
It's the biggest by far,
It's the sun!

Alice Schaale (8)
The Raleigh School

The Ghost I Welcomed As A Host

I really met a ghost
I welcomed it as a host
    At the dining table
    With my Auntie Mabel.
She didn't like it much
Neither did I as such
    I chucked him out
    Then I found out
That my Auntie Mabel was dead.

I brought the ghost in
We made an awful din
And the neighbours complained about their heads.

Mary Lawton (9)
The Raleigh School

My Xbox

Switch it on
Grab a controller
Rev it up
Red light, green light - go!

Racing, skating, running, shooting, boarding, footballing
Each time something different
I'm behind
I'm in front
Make that turn
Shoot that man
Score that goal
Closer and closer the finish line
I've lost
I've won
Time's up
Let's go again
Rev it up . . .

Dominic Hunt (9)
The Raleigh School

Flowers

Flowers are different colours
And have a lovely scent,
No other plant is like them,
They are Heaven-sent.

The colors of the flowers
Are red, white, green and blue
And if you really love someone,
They might give some to you.

The bluebells in the spring
Are such lovely things,
They give me so much pleasure,
When I walk in the sunny weather.

Amy Patching (8)
The Raleigh School

Fireworks

Fireworks, fireworks,
You glisten in the sky,
So colourful,
I don't want you to end.

Fireworks, fireworks,
You are so lovely and bright,
You make me feel
Tingly inside.

I love you oh fireworks
And I don't want you to go.
Catherine wheel, oh Catherine wheel,
You swirl around and around,
How you are ever so bright,
You're as bright as the sun.

Hanna Greenstreet (8)
The Raleigh School

Bruno Is My Dog

Bruno is my dog
The best dog
The bouncy dog
He is reddish gold
And so, so bold
And never does as he is told
But he is only 7 months old.

Bruno is my dog
He bites your arm
But means no harm
He howls to the sound of his squeaky toy
And always has to jump up to a girl or boy.

Bruno is my dog
He loves to play
And does as he may
But never shall he leave my side
Oh! Bruno is my dog!

Rhiannon Davies (9)
The Raleigh School

The Little Acorn

An acorn falls from a tree
And gets picked up by a bee.

The acorn gets carried to a wood,
Where a hundred oak trees stood.

A squirrel came scampering along the way
And found the acorn where it lay.

He buried it deep for his winter snack,
But a memory he did lack.

And so the acorn met the spring,
With a tall and slender,
Green unfurling . . .

Alex Davies (9)
The Raleigh School

Poaching

What's the point of poaching?
It's just a waste of time.
All it's about is money,
It's always been a crime.

They're killing off all the animals,
Soon they will be extinct,
The gun will go bang!
After will be their last blink.

If people weren't so greedy,
Wanting animal skins,
There wouldn't be orphan babies,
The meat wouldn't go into tins.

We want to stop the poaching,
What's the point of killing?
What's the harm they've done to us?
It gives us all a chilling.

Charlotte Merry (8)
The Raleigh School

Summer Hours

I'm lying on the beach
With the sun shining over me
And an umbrella for shade.

My pond is bubbling and boiling with fishes
Swimming around quiet and tranquil
Blue to the ground.

The sky is clear
With the sun shining down
The air is clean and fresh.

Charlie Holland (10)
The Raleigh School

The Party

The animals were having a party,
George Giraffe came long and tall,
Hippy Hippo came fat and plump
And Sammy Spider was tiny and small.

When the crazy games began,
Charley the Cheetah ran so fast.
Jumping gazelles leapt over a very big can
And in the race the elephant was last.

A slithery snake swallowed frogs whole,
The howler monkeys howled for their food.
Some tigers fed on a chunk of meat,
As the lion sat in a grumpy mood.

Leaving the party they waved goodbye,
They trotted home one by one,
Wondering and hoping there'd be another,
As the night was brilliant fun.

Tarun Aluvihare (9)
The Raleigh School

My Brother

I have a little brother
Who drives me mad,
He can be very sweet
But also very bad.

He throws all my things about
And sometimes screams and shouts,
He often wakes me up at night
But really - he's alright.

Jadesola Crundwell (8)
The Raleigh School

Pandas

Pandas are big and black and white,
They love to eat all day and all night.
Pandas live far away
And sleep for twenty three hours a day.
Pandas are cute and cuddly too,
They live in a den and eat bamboo.
They are endangered I'm sad to say,
Maybe they'll be gone one day.
Pandas are my favourite creature,
In my room they're quite a feature.
There are pandas in every place,
In my bed there's not much space.
I have nine cuddly panda toys,
Some are girls and some are boys.
I cuddle them when I turn off the light,
They keep me safe every night.
I'd love to see a real panda someday,
No matter how much I have to pay.
It's something I've always wanted to do,
That's my dream, maybe it will come true.

Amy de Beaux (8)
The Raleigh School

Friendship

Sometimes when I'm feeling down,
Across my face there is a frown.
When my friends come to me and say,
'You're not needed here anyway.'
But soon after we all say sorry
And I realise there was no need to worry!

Zoella Zaborski (10)
The Raleigh School

My Mouth And The Marshmallow

My dear, my dear marshmallow,
Your centre oh so gooey,
You're covered with dainty, light sugar.

My dear, my dear marshmallow,
You're made of magical frosting,
By jove, you're only costing me one, twenty, my dream.

My dear, my dear marshmallow,
How I long to touch your lips,
It's far better than eating biscuits, you really are the tops.

My dear, my dear marshmallow,
We shall be melted as one,
Then you and me will come on our honey-marsh-moon together.

My dear, my dear marshmallow,
We shall go past Jelly Tot town, then straight down
And into Land Lollypop, that's our stop.

My dear, my dear marshmallow,
Time's up, not chosen, well fiddle-dee-dee,
Tough luck, you're in my lunch box for tea.

Freya Bromley (9)
The Raleigh School

Water

Rushing, gushing from the falls,
Fizzing, whizzing into pools,
Bashing, crashing around rocks,
Driving boats in and out of docks,
Sparkling, dazzling salty seas,
Enabling plants, humans and trees,
    Streams to rivers,
    Rivers to seas,
    Splashing waves,
    Calm breeze.

Anna Robinson (9)
The Raleigh School

Our Beach

Skipping under a tunnel of trees
Cool and damp,
Sun glistening through the leaves
Running down the wide open field, hair flying,
Wow! What a view!

Skidding down the steep, wiggling path
Butterflies fluttering on their delicate wings,
Stripy bees buzz round a circle of flowers
Not long to go to our beach below!

Splashing about in foamy waves
Wading up to our knees,
Feet sinking in soft, silky sand
Glittering fish swim away from our toes.

Boats in the distance float calmly away
Seagulls soaring across the clear blue sky,
Sun shining on the silvery sea
No one else here but Mum, Dad
And us three!

Our very special beach.

Ellie Silvey (9)
The Raleigh School

A Sudden Shower

Clouds come in purple, blue and black
Lowering the ceiling of the sky
I shelter from within my treehouse
Acorns fall down with allied drops
You hear the rustle of the rushing rain
Slowly clouds clear, rain drains
The sun fights back again.

Edward Baker (9)
The Raleigh School

My Solar System Poem

When you go to planet Mars,
You will see a lot of stars.

Uranus is between Neptune and Saturn,
I don't think it has a lovely pattern.

Jupiter has a lot of moons,
None of which would fit on spoons.

Pluto is a long way away,
I don't think you will get there today.

Mercury is nearest to the sun,
But I don't think you will have much fun.

Venus is quite close to us,
But we don't make much of a fuss.

Saturn has a lot of rings,
Dust and ice and lots of things.

Neptune has a lot of water,
But I don't really think it oughta.

Earth is where we live today,
My poem is finished, hip hip hooray.

Cameron Smith (8)
The Raleigh School